COMMUNISM IN THE BIBLE

Communism in the Bible

JOSÉ PORFIRIO MIRANDA

*Translated from the Spanish
by Robert R. Barr*

ORBIS BOOKS
Maryknoll, New York 10545

Originally published as *Comunismo en la Biblia,* copyright © 1981 by Siglo Veintiuno Editores, S.A., Cerro del Agua 248, Mexico 20, D.F.

This translation copyright © 1982 by Orbis Books, Maryknoll, NY 10545

Library of Congress Cataloging in Publication Data

Miranda, José Porfirio.
    Communism in the Bible

    Translation of: Comunismo en la Biblia.
    Bibliography: p.
    Includes index.
    1. Sociology, Biblical. 2. Communism and
Christianity—Biblical teaching. I. Title.
    BS670.M5513   261.8   81-16936
    ISBN 0-88344-014-8 (pbk.)   AACR2

"All whose faith had drawn them together held everything in common: they would sell their property and possessions and make a general distribution as the need of each required" (Acts 2:44–45).

CONTENTS

FOREWORD

This is a manifesto. But it is a biblical manifesto, which submits to all the rigor of scientific exegesis and accepts its challenge. If the thesis is not demonstrated by meticulous scholarship, consider the thesis unposited. Precisely what this book recriminates in official theology is the lucubration of a whole concept of Christianity independently of the Bible and even in contradiction to it. Accordingly this book claims no more validity than its demonstrations force upon it.

The present work deepens the investigation undertaken in both of my previous exegetical works, *Marx and the Bible* and *Being and the Messiah*. But it does not logically presuppose them. I have taken care to place it on its own footing. In fact, in spite of the reduced format with a view to wider diffusion, I have sharpened certain of the analyses I began in those two stout volumes, in particular the Prophets, the Psalms, and the authentic logia and historical deeds of Jesus of Nazareth. This book is concise, but it is the fruit of many years of research.

My political conclusion has no need of words to belabor it. The title of the book puts it in relief. I repeat, this is a manifesto. And it seeks to make itself heard by all the poor of the earth.

ABBREVIATIONS

A   Codex Alexandrinus

ATD   *Das Alte Testament Deutsch*. Göttingen: Vanden-hoeck.

B   Codex Vaticanus

LTK   *Lexikon für Theologie und Kirche*. Freiburg: Herder, 1957–1968.

MEW   *Marx-Engels Werke*. Berlin: Dietz, 1955–1973.

NTD   *Das Neue Testament Deutsch*. Göttingen: Vanden-hoeck.

PL   *Patrologiae cursus . . . Series latina.*

PG   *Patrologiae cursus . . . Series graeca.*

S   Codex Sinaiticus

TWNT   *Theologisches Wörterbuch zum Neuen Testament*. Stuttgart: Kohlhammer, 1933–1978.

CHAPTER ONE

CHRISTIANITY IS COMMUNISM

For a Christian to say he or she is anti-Marxist is understandable. There are numerous varieties of Marxism, and it is possible that our Christian is referring to one of the many materialistic philosophies which style themselves Marxist without having much at all to do with Marx.

For a Christian to claim to be not only anti-Marxist but anti-Marx as well, it is probably owing to not having read all of Marx, and the repugnance is a symptom of simple ignorance. But when all is said and done I do not really care. I am under no obligation to defend Marx.

But for a Christian to claim to be anticommunist is quite a different matter, and without doubt constitutes the greatest scandal of our century. It is not a good thing to weigh a book down with cries and shouts, but someone finally has to voice the most obvious and important truths, which no one mentions as if everyone knew them.

The notion of communism is in the New Testament, right down to the letter—and so well put that in the twenty centuries since it was written no one has come up with a better definition of communism than Luke in Acts 2:44–45 and 4:32–35. In fact, the definition Marx borrowed from Louis Blanc, "From each one according to his capacities, to each one according to his needs," is inspired by, if not directly copied from, Luke's formulation eighteen centuries earlier. There is no clearer demonstration of the brainwashing to which the establishment keeps us subjected than the officially promulgated conception of Christianity as anticommunist.

At this moment two-thirds of Latin America writhes under the yoke of atrocious anticommunist dictatorships. Nearly all the rest of Latin America suffers from a most ill-concealed anticommunist repression. The international politics of nearly all the countries of the world, and their consequent criminal armament ideology, rallies to this contradictory watchword: "Defend Christian civilization from communism!" At such a moment there are no words adequate to this other cry: But what if, in the history of the West, it is Christianity that *started* communism? What if, from the first century to the nineteenth, groups of Christians were never lacking who, in spite of repression by the established powers and by the church, vigorously advocated communism, Bible in hand! What manner of insanity has swooped down on the Western world that it combats the Christian project *par excellence* as if it were its greatest enemy?

1. Intentional Misunderstandings

Ultimately the Marxists have been doing us a favor by propagating the idea of communism in our absence—our culpable absence. But to identify communism with Marxism implies a crass ignorance of history. It is far from certain that the establishment is struggling against atheistic materialism, as the powerful tell themselves in order to tranquillize their consciences. This repressive struggle of theirs dates from much earlier. It existed for many centuries when no communist was a materialist and no communist was an atheist; it existed when materialism and atheism did not even exist. Marxism is a mere episode in the history of the communist project. The pope and the other powerful ones are not fighting atheism, but us, who are Christians, who believe in God and Jesus, and who only want to see the gospel become reality.

Surely there are different interpretations of the gospel, and the purpose of this book is to air them. But then the powerful are attacking an interpretation of the Bible different from their own. This onslaught of theirs is nothing but the continuation of what they were carrying on all through the Middle Ages and the first three centuries of the modern era. The denunciation of materialism is a mere pretext for anticommunist persecution. If these gentlemen did not have this pretext they would invent another— as in fact they did throughout the Middle Ages, with different pretexts in the sixteenth century, and still others in the seventeenth and eighteenth centuries. If materialism were the reason for the anticommunist persecution, how do you explain the fact that they persecuted communism long before materialism existed? No, what they persecute and repress is communism as such. But the communist project is explicitly defended in the Bible as proper to and characteristic of Christianity. It was invented neither by the Marxists nor by the medieval or modern Christian groups!

When the official doctrinal propaganda asserts that the communist idea is inseparable from materialist ideologies, it is denying facts as evident and inconcealable as daylight. In primitive Christianity, and for eighteen centuries after, the communist idea existed without materialism of any kind. And even today, what logical relationship can be pointed out between "having everything in common" (Acts 2:44) and denying the existence or efficacy of the spirit? The truth is precisely the reverse: communism cannot be actualized unless we recognize the infinite respect due God in each of our neighbors, including those who are economically unproductive by weakness or age or natural gifts. The failure of Russian communism is the evidence. (What you now have in the Soviet Union is state capitalism.)

Then why does official Christianity make war on an idea that is expressly sponsored in the fonts of Christianity, and which, logically, can only be brought to realization on the basis of authentic Christianity? The denial of the existence of the spirit is far more inseparable from each one's selfishly seeking his or her own proper advantage and gain, as capitalism teaches us to do. The thesis that communism cannot be separated from materialism is one of those monstrous Hitler-style falsehoods that are proclaimed with all the greater aplomb the more false they are.

Examined objectively, it is the diametrical inversion of the real facts.

Another deliberate misunderstanding is the allegation that we Christian communists are only being fashionable, or adapting to progressive currents, or zealously keeping up to date. In the name of my Latin American brothers and sisters I here formally declare that we are shameless conservatives. We are looking for the literal gospel. We detest that opportunist principle according to which Christianity ought constantly to adapt and accommodate to changing circumstances. As if Christianity had no content of its own to proclaim and actualize! We reject the feebleminded notion that Christianity must be Roman in Roman imperial times, feudal in the Middle Ages, absolutist during the monarchy, liberal for the French Revolution, and so on. We leave such flexibility to a church which, for many centuries now, has considered it of no importance to verify objectively what it is that Christ wanted to bring about in the world. It is those who repress us who are being "fashionable"—those who are anticommunist by adaptation to the Trilateral Commission and the Chase Manhattan Bank. We, on the contrary, believe that Jesus Christ came to save the world, not to adapt to the world. And they say we are the ones who run after the current fashion?—we who accept no other criterion than the one formulated in the first century in the fonts of Christianity?

They can likewise lay aside the notion that, while not actually denying the existence of Spirit, we care more for the material than for the spiritual. But in the first place, the final criterion established and left us by Jesus as the *only one* is, "I was hungry and you gave me to eat; I was thirsty and you gave me to drink, was a stranger and you took me in, was stripped naked and you clothed me; sick and you visited me, imprisoned and you came to see me" (Matt. 25:35-36). If this is preoccupying oneself more with the material than with the spiritual, then the self-styled official spiritualism ought to stop beating about the bush and direct its accusations against Jesus himself. Here we see all over again that the confrontation is between two interpretations of the Bible, not between Christians and atheists. And the difference is that we take the message of Jesus literally and without gloss.

But in the second place, is unrestricted fidelity to Jesus Christ to be reproached as preoccupation with the material? How are we going to give food to all who are hungry if we leave the means of production in private hands, which *necessarily* destine these means to the augmentation of capital and not to the satisfaction of the needs of the population? Do the official theologians really think they can maintain that there is more spirituality in the escapist selfishness of people who tranquillize themselves by saying, "There have always been people who starved to death, we are not divine providence," than in the decision of the people who want to be faithful to Jesus by undertaking all possible means to give food to the hungry, knowing that they are exposing themselves to repression, prison, and torture? Is there less spirituality in ruining one's future and social prestige by taking Jesus seriously than in adapting to the sweet enchantment of a bourgeoisie singing "I am dedicated to spiritual things"?

Furthermore, they can lay aside the notion that, while not actually denying the existence of God, we care more about human beings than about God. We have dedicated our lives to Jesus. Don't these theologians think Jesus is God? And this is where the antirevolutionary onslaught smites the essential point, the very essence of biblical revelation. Let it be clearly understood: the one thing the Christian revolutionaries advocate and defend is the adoration of the true God, in contrast with the adoration of idols, which for many centuries now has been inculcated by a theology radically ignorant of the Bible. This is not a theme that can simply be listed as item number so-and-so in a list of objections. It is not even just a theme. It is the one single motive of our rebellion, and the one single content of our theology. We have never pretended to do more than *theo*-logy, in the strict and literal sense of the word.

The God of the Bible is not knowable directly. The idols are. And the mental idols are more important than the material ones. There are those who believe that the only thing they have to do is put the word "God" in their minds to be directed toward the true God. But this is what the Bible fights to the death. The god of these adorers is a concept within their minds. With this intramental act they fail to transcend their own subjectivity, their own psychism, their own *I*. Either the true God is transcendent or the true God does not exist. The otherness constituted by the oppressed neighbor, who calls on our aid seeking justice, bursts our solipsism asunder. This is the only way we transcend ourselves. The God of the Bible is knowable only in otherness, in the call for help of the poor, the orphan, the widow, the stranger. Our revolutionary message has this objective only: that all people may come to know the one true God, and knowing God be saved. Those who accuse us of preferring the human to the divine are not only committing calumny; they are above all committing ignorance—supine ignorance of the Bible itself.

Last, they can abandon the notion that we care more for the transformation of structures than for the transformation of persons, that we care more for the social than for the personal. The contrary is the truth. Our revolution is directed toward the creation of the new human being. But unlike the attackers, we seek to posit the necessary means for the formation of this new human being. And the indispensable means is a new social structure. Is it not perfectly obvious that an existing social system has more efficacy for education or miseducation than the exhortations of classroom or temple? How far can you get with the idea that a person should not place his or her heart in money and material things (the central idea of the Sermon on the Mount) if the existing social system inculcates just the contrary under pain of blows and death? Perhaps an insignificant minority can heroically resist the peremptory mandates of such a system. But Christianity cares about all human beings. It cannot content itself with saving a tiny minority. The majority cannot even assign a sense of realism to the Christian message of brotherhood and solidarity with neighbor, when the social structure imposes upon it, under pain of annihilation, the task of seeking its proper interest and letting the chips fall where they may, without preoccupying itself with other people. Structural change will be a mere means for personal change—but a means so obviously necessary, that those who fail to give it first priority demonstrate by that very fact that their vaunted desire to transform persons is just empty rhetoric.

To return to where we began, the five establishment pretexts for their unscrupulous crusade against communism are mere diversionary maneuvers: identifying communism with materialism and atheism, accusing us of chasing mode and fashion, imputing to us a lack of spirituality, alleging we care more for human beings than for God, and attributing to us a greater preoccupation with structures than with persons. It is time to drop all these side issues and concentrate on the fundamental fact: the Bible teaches communism.

2. Original Christianity

> All the believers together had everything in common; they sold their possessions and their goods, and distributed among all in accordance with each one's need [Acts 2:44–45].

> The heart of the multitude of believers was one and their soul was one, and not a single one said anything of what he had was his, but all things were in common. . . . There was no poor person among them, since whoever possessed fields or houses sold them, bore the proceeds of the sale and placed them at the feet of the apostles; and a distribution was made to each one in accordance with his need [Acts 4:32, 34–35].

Luke's normative intention stands out. There is no question of a special lifestyle that could be considered peculiar to some Christians in contrast with the general mass of Christians. His insistence on the universality of communism from a literary point of view is even a little affected—*pántes hoi pisteúsantes* (2:44), all the believers, all who had believed in Jesus Christ, all Christians; *oudè heîs* (4:32), not a single one said anything was his; *hósoi ktétores* (4:34), whoever possessed fields or houses, whoever had anything. If they wanted to be Christians the condition was communism.

The anticommunist commentators allege that this is Luke's personal point of view, and that the other New Testament writers fail to corroborate it. The argument is invalid, because none of the other writers describes the life of original Christianity, and hence there is no document upon which one could base an attempt to give Luke the lie. But let us suppose (not concede) that some other New Testament author were to differ with Luke; how would this justify the persecution (styling itself "Christian") of a social project that is explicitly and repeatedly promoted by one of the principal authors of the New Testament?

We shall see that the hypothesis is false, for Jesus himself was a communist. But let us place ourselves hypothetically in the worst possible position: that only Luke teaches communism. With what right, indeed with what elemental logic, is it thereupon asserted that communism is incompatible with Christianity? Does not the very fact that they make this assertion demonstrate that the anti-communists who call themselves Christians are alienated and are merely claiming Christianity when in reality they are being moved by an anti-Christian motivation of which they are unaware? If at least the Lucan part of the New Testament teaches communism, how is it possible to maintain that communism is at odds with Christianity?

Let us suppose (not concede) that there are parts of the New Testament which lend footing to the projection of social systems different from Luke's. Well and good. That some Christians to-day may prefer these other parts of the Bible to Luke's is their affair. But with what right do they deny the name Christian to what the Lucan part of the Bible teaches emphatically and re-peatedly? The origin of the communist idea in the history of the West is the New Testament, not Jamblichus or Plato. The banner the communist groups and movements marched under—from the first century through the Middle Ages all the way to Wilhelm Weitling (1808–1871), in whose procommunist organization Marx and Engels were active in their youth (cf. *MEW* 17:485)—was the New Testament, not *The Republic* or the *Vita Pythagorae*. The ruthless repression of the communists in the name of Christianity for the last seventeen centuries is a farce, and the most grotesque falsification that can be imagined.

A second anticommunist allegation against the texts we have cited from Luke is: The communism of the first Christians failed. It is flabbergasting that sermons, documents of the magisterium, books, and bourgeois public opinion should brook the notion that this is an argument. The Sermon on the Mount failed too, but this does not deprive it of its normative character. In the clear intention of the original report, communism is obligatory for Christians. This is not modified, not in the slightest, by the fact of a failure of the original communist intent. What should concern us is to find out why it broke down, and bring communism to realization without committing whatever error caused the first Christians to break down. This would be the only logical conclusion if our objectors had the flimsiest desire to be guided by the Bible. But what our objectors have done is make an antecedent and irreformable decision to disagree with the Bible, and to this purpose they bring forward every pretext, even if it tramples upon the most elemental logic.

To cite that initial failure is pure pretext. It is as if we told ourselves we were eliminating the Ten Commandments because they failed in history. The establishment theologians confound the normative with the factual—and they confound them deliberately, in order to be able to disagree with any biblical teaching for which they have no taste. This is anti-Christianity, disguised as "Christian civilization" for the purpose of rejecting the gospel.

According to Marx (*MEW* 18:160) the cause of the failure was that the first Christians neglected the political struggle. We shall speak of the political order in another chapter. Personally I think that a communist island in an economic sea characterized by the exploitation of some persons by others cannot be maintained, and that this is why the first Christian communism failed. That is, as we have said above, the surrounding, involving social system has far more power than exhortations have. The communism of the first Christians failed because the first Christians were very few. But today we Christians are the majority in the West and the principal force in the world.

There is a third charge made against the communism of the first Christians. But the reader has already perceived that this whole cascade of objections, one replacing another as each turns out absurd, is only a series of emotional symptoms proceeding from the objectants' instinctive repugnance to the message of the Bible. The third objection runs as follows: the communism of the first Christians was optional as can be seen from Peter's words to Ananias, "Was it not still yours if you kept it, and once you sold it was it not yours to dispose of?" (Acts 5:4). One would love to know what cohesion there is among these objections. First they were saying that Luke is lying; then that he is not lying, but that the project collapsed; and finally, not only is he not lying, but his report is so reliable that they are going to use Acts 5:4 to beat communism. It is plain to see that the so-called objections are just irrational reactions, the spasms of an uncontrollable visceral revulsion.

Still, let us examine the convulsion as if it were an objection. It is astonishing that there was ever considered to be any validity in this third charge. Let us take, hypothetically, the worst possible position. Let us suppose (falsely, as we shall see) that according to Luke, communism was *optional*. I answer: But you combat it as if it were *evil*! According to yourselves, the Bible (merely) *recommends* it; so you *prohibit* it!

"Optional" ought to mean that we Christians may opt for it. Nevertheless you persecute, as seditious, criminal, and anti-Christian, whoever opts for communism. I have never seen anything more distracted and demented. To forbid communism they bend all their efforts to prove the Bible recommends it.

But the hypothesis is false. According to Luke, what is optional is not communism, but Christianity. Peter does not tell Ananias that he could have come into the Christian community without renouncing the private ownership of his goods. Nor could he say such a thing after it was explicitly emphasized that of the Christians "*not a single one* said anything was his" (Acts 4:32). Ananias lied to the Holy Spirit by pretending to become a Christian *via* a simulated renunciation.

The objection belongs to the type of reader who thinks a work can be understood without understanding the thought of the author. Luke would have to have been a very slow-witted writer if he claimed to assert, in the Ananias episode (Acts 5:1–11), the optional character of communism, when four verses earlier (4:34) he has insisted that "*whoever* possessed fields or houses sold them," and so on, and two verses above that, "and *not a single one* said anything was his" (4:32), and still earlier, "*all the faithful together* had everything in common" (2:44). This is the Luke who had placed these words on the lips of Jesus: "*Every one* of you who does not renounce all he has cannot be my disciple" (Luke 14:33); and now the rightists would have it that according to Luke one can be a disciple of Christ without renouncing all one has. What they ought to be doing is rejecting Luke as a jabbering cheat. But to assert that according to Luke one can be a Christian without renouncing private property is an insolent rejection of the documentation which all of us have right before our eyes.

Let it be well noted that the last verse cited is concerned with the simple fact of being disciples of Christ, and not of some "special vocation" or other. See the beginning of the pericope: "Many crowds accompanied him, and he, turning, said to them: . . ." (Luke 14:25). He is not addressing the Twelve, but the crowd. It is a simple matter of the conditions for being a Christian, exactly as in the texts we cited from Acts. What is optional is to be a Christian, to be a disciple of Christ. Those who wrest the Ananias episode from its context are trying to read it as if it had no author, as if no one had written it. As Hinkelammert has said, this episode means: pain of death for whoever betrays communism, Christianity's indispensable condition.

But the most curious and paradoxical thing about the objection we have just been considering is that it supposes that *our* communism is not optional, or that the communism of Marx is not optional. With supreme fury it attacks a nonexistent enemy. Never have we thought that communism can be realized except by free decision of the workers, rural people, and unemployed, who together form the immense majority of the population. And Marx thought the same.

It must be taken into account that a system is a system. Let it not be thought that we in capitalism are outside all systems, although this is the absurdity which, at bottom, the objection assumes. It is impossible that, within one and the same country, the criteria for the destination of its resources be the satisfaction of the needs of the population, and at the same time be to make profit for capital. Either the system is capitalist or the system is communist. Those who wish that communism be optional for the capitalists are preventing it from being an option for the vast majority of the population. So where does that leave us? They wanted it to be optional, did they not?

It is preposterous to suppose that the proletariat are in capitalism by free decision—or that capitalism is a kind of point zero, the "natural" situation imposed on no one, and that only if you want to move from this point does the dilemma arise of doing so either by free option or by a constraint that violates your freedom.

The *real* dilemma is this one: either practically the whole population imposes communism upon an insignificant minority, or a handful of persons imposes capitalism on practically the whole population. Those who love freedom must choose between *these* alternatives. There is no third way. In one country there cannot be more than one system, precisely because it is a system. The illusory "mixed economy" is capitalism; the state firms have to obey the rules of capitalism and become the pawn of the private firms.

Where would the capitalists get the human resources to run their factories if the workers of the country were to opt for a communist system? Let us suppose that a communist revolution leaves the capitalists in freedom of option. To whom will they sell their products if the population wishes to have nothing to do with capitalist production? The theoreticians who seek freedom of option even for the insignificant minority are closing their eyes to the fact that this freedom of option cannot exist without eliminating freedom of option for the vast majority. Here it can be seen how much they really love freedom. They want the freedom to deprive everyone else of freedom.

It is what the objectants *suppose* that is most false in all of this—that the proletariat are in capitalism by free decision. But in order to have freedom there must be a knowledge of the alternatives. If all ideological sources, including the church, television, and films, characterize the communist idea as satanic, criminal, and anti-Christian, what freedom of option do the proletariat have?

3. The Kingdom Is on Earth

Now let us investigate whether the first Christians invented their communism, or based it upon the teachings of Jesus and the whole biblical tradition. In other words, our task is to extend our vision beyond the book called *The Acts of the Apostles*. And here we begin to specify the moral and obligatory reason for communism. But as we are going to base our discussion primarily upon three authentic logia of Jesus concerning the kingdom of God, and inasmuch as the supposition that the kingdom is in the other world has prevented so many from understanding these statements, we must prefix an explanation—of paramount importance of itself, but, from the viewpoint of the logical thread of this book, having the character of a prenote.

To begin, let us compare Matthew 13:11 ("To you has been given to know the mysteries of the kingdom of the Heavens") on the one hand, with Mark 4:11 ("To you has been given the mystery of the kingdom of God") and Luke 8:10 ("To you has been given to know the mysteries of the kingdom of God") on the other.

Also, compare Matthew 3:2 ("The kingdom of the Heavens has come") on one hand, with Mark 1:15 ("The kingdom of God has come") and Luke 10:9 ("The kingdom of God has come to you") on the other.

This is a sample. We could lengthen the list of comparisons between the text of Matthew and the texts of Mark and Luke. Scholars agree that Matthew systematically substitutes "kingdom of the heavens" for the original "kingdom of God," and have inquired into the reason for this systematic editorial modification.

They also agree on the answer. This is important to emphasize. All the exegetes who broach the subject, be they conservatives or liberals, those of an otherworldly penchant or those of an earthly, explain the editorial phenomenon by the late Judaic custom of avoiding all explicit use of the name "God." People said "the heavens," or even "the Name," instead of saying "God." It was believed that this constituted obedience to the commandment of the decalogue forbidding taking the name of God in vain. Today this respect seems excessive to us, and even Christ did not observe it. But the literary fact cannot be denied. It is superabundantly documented in the rabbinical writings of the first century B.C. and the first century of the Christian era. Even today in our Western languages there are vestiges, as when we say "Heaven help us" when what we really mean is "God help us."

And so there is no question of Matthew's placing the kingdom in the other world. He simply uses the habitual circumlocution of late Judaism to avoid as much as possible mentioning the name of God. The editor we call Matthew (who is surely not the apostle) either introduced this circumlocution himself or found it in the writings he utilized in redacting his Gospel. And where there is special motive, the motive warrants the exception.

As to where the kingdom is to be realized, Matthew has no doubts. In the parable of the weeds (Matt. 13:24–30, 36–43), which is a parable about the kingdom, he says expressly that "the field is the world" (v. 38), and at the end of the story he does not say that the kingdom will be transferred to some other place but that "the Son of Man will send his angels, who will remove from his kingdom all scandals and all workers of iniquity" (v. 41), and that then "the just will shine like the sun in the kingdom of their Father" (v. 43).

And so for Matthew too, just as for all the other known sacred authors, in the Old Testament as in the New, the kingdom is on earth. Now, the Matthean expression "the kingdom of the heavens" was the only one serving the escapist theologians as pretext for maintaining that the kingdom was to be realized in the other world. Not even texts about glory or entering into glory provided them any support, for the Psalms explicitly teach, "Salvation surrounds those who fear him, so that the glory will dwell in our land" (Ps. 85:10).

Of course the Matthean circumlocution "of the heavens" was only a pretext. If they had not been blinded by the scorn their escapist theology holds for our world, they could have seen where the kingdom is right from the Psalter. For instance, Psalm 74, wholly dedicated to "Yahweh my king from olden time" (v. 12), whose rule consists in saving "the poor and the needy" (v. 21), ends by begging Yahweh to attack all oppressors (vv. 22–23), since he must "make salvation real in the midst of the earth" (v. 12). And Psalm 10 proclaims, looking into the future, "Yahweh is king eternally and for ever, the gentiles have been swept from their land" (v. 16). They could have found the same thing throughout Chapter 32 of Isaiah, in Psalm 146, and in hundreds of other Old Testament texts.

But there is no demonstration of this blindness to equal the fact that the theologians are not even impressed by the prayer which Christ taught us and which they pray every day—"Thy kingdom come" (Matt. 6:10, Luke 11:2). He does not say, "Take us to your kingdom," but "your kingdom come." Where is it to come if not to the earth, which is where we are when we say "come"? That the escapists do not read the Psalter carefully is a frequent fault of theirs, though it ought not to be; but that they pay no attention even to the Lord's Prayer is really the height of blindness.

Furthermore, not just a part of the content, but *the* content of the "good news" Jesus proclaimed, that is, the content of the gospel in the strict sense, is, "the kingdom has come" (Mark 1:15 and parallels). Where can it have come if not to earth? Besides,

Jesus says "the kingdom of God has come to you" (Luke 11:20, Matt. 12:28); the only possible meaning is that it has come to the earth on which those to whom Jesus says "has come to you" are standing. Accordingly, to maintain that the kingdom is in the other world is equivalent to denying the very content of the gospel. And to say in escapist desperation that the kingdom is "partly in this world and partly in the other" is to launch a thesis totally without support in Jesus' teaching.

Even the Book of Revelation, which talks of nothing but the heavenly Jerusalem, finally tells us: "And I saw the holy city, the new Jerusalem, coming down from heaven from God" (Rev. 21:2); "and I was shown the holy city, Jerusalem, descending from the sky, from God" (Rev. 21:10). The kingdom is made ready in heaven, or resides temporarily in heaven, but its final destination is earth. Hence the visionary says he "saw it coming down," since it is on earth that it is to be established. He had already told us, "And he made them to be a kingdom, and priests for our God, and they will reign over all the earth" (Rev. 5:10), and at the end of the book he adds, "And they shall reign for ever and ever" (Rev. 22:5). If he expressly says that the kingdom or reign will be over the earth, it becomes idle to inquire where the new Jerusalem descends to as it "comes down from heaven."

Our reference to the Book of Revelation in this context is important, since in 2:7 this book mentions the word "paradise." And this, erroneously, has been seen as the ace in the hole for the escapists. First, though, let us note once more that the kingdom of God is on earth, as is demonstrated by the texts we have cited, and that on this point there is not the least wavering on the part of the sacred authors. Hence what paradise might be, or being with Christ, or Abraham's bosom, or the heavenly treasure, is a question we could well leave aside, because what matters to us is the definitive kingdom, which constitutes the central content of the message of Jesus. The escapists can have paradise. But the passages cited from Revelation give the same key as the most competent researchers (Strack-Billerweck and Joachim Jeremias) have found in the copious Judaic documentation.

Without using the term paradise, in Revelation the garden of God appears as a summation of the glory and of the fullness: Revelation describes the final Jerusalem as paradise when it speaks of the trees of life and the water of life (22:1; cf. 22:14,19), the destruction of the serpent of old (20:2; cf. 20:10), the elimination of suffering, of need, and of death (21:4). The place of residence of the definitive paradise is, according to 21:2,10, the Jerusalem of the renewed earth [J. Jeremias, *TWNT* 5:767].

Paradise is Jerusalem, provisionally heavenly, which will at last descend from heaven and be installed on our earth for ever and ever. According to the Bible, situations outside our world are transitory and temporary, whether they are known as paradise, or the bosom of Abraham, or heavenly treasure, or being with Christ, or third heaven. As the New Testament employs the terminology of contemporary Judaism, and as the latter offers abundant documentation, scholars have not entertained the least doubt in the matter.

For example the Lucan parable of the rich man and Lazarus (Luke 16:19–31) typically places the rich man in *hádes* (v. 23), which is the technical name for the place of torment after the death of the unjust, in contrast with *géenna*, the definitive place of torment after the final judgment (cf. Strack-Billerbeck, 2:228 and 4:1040—the same terminology as in Testamentum Abrahae 20 A and 4 Esd. 7:85,93). "Abraham's bosom" (Luke 16:22), used in conjunction and contrast with *hádes*, is equally provisional, until such time as the kingdom is realized, including the resurrection of the dead.

In like fashion, Matthew 5:12 does not say, You shall receive much recompense in the heavens, but "Your recompense is great in heaven," which is the place where it is provisorily kept. Theodor Zahn comments: "After the beatitudes of Matthew 5:3–10, it is obvious that the reward (mentioned in 5:12) will be given to the disciples only in the kingdom which is to be established on earth" (*Das Evangelium des Matthäus*, p. 197). And indeed there cannot be the shadow of a doubt in this respect, as Matthew has just said of the generous that "they shall inherit the earth" (5:5). The idea in Matthew 5:12 is the same as in Acts 10:4: "Your prayers and your alms have arisen as a reminder before the presence of God." This same idea is found in Tobit 12:12–15.

Likewise the conversation of the crucified Christ with the good thief demonstrates precisely the contrary of what escapist theology would like it to. "When you come to your kingdom" is in deliberate contrast with "This very day . . . in paradise" (Luke 23:42–43). Jesus does not deny that it is only later that he will come into his kingdom—but he wishes to have the good thief in his company right from today. Evidently, paradise, as in all the literature of that time, is a provisional place, pending the arrival of the moment in which the Messiah comes to his kingdom— which is surely on the earth, since the good thief is on the earth when he says "when you come."

Well and good, but it is not to be thought that an interpretation of the Bible is a conceptual construct, which each scholar invents according to his or her mentality, and which is presented alongside other interpretations for the public to choose the one it finds most suitable. To speak of a kingdom of God in the other world is not only to found a new religion without any relationship with the teaching of Christ (for none of the texts wielded by escapist theology mentions the kingdom); it is to assert exactly the contrary of what Christ teaches: "The kingdom has come to you," and "Your kingdom come." The fact that tradition has taught for centuries that the kingdom is in the other world only demonstrates that that tradition betrayed Jesus and founded another religion completely different.

This concludes the explanation of our third point. It was a necessary pre-note for what is about to follow. But consider the importance it has in itself: the conservatives' resistance to the elimination of private property in the kingdom of God depends on where you situate the kingdom. This is truly prodigious inconsistency. If the kingdom is in heaven, they accept the texts abolishing private property in the kingdom. If the kingdom is on earth, they deny that these same texts abolish private property. Evidently, they cannot maintain that private property persists in heaven. But according to Jesus, what they think is in heaven is really on earth. To doubt this they have to deny the Lord's Prayer and the central and single content of the good news, of the gospel. We leave it to the reader to judge how they can conscientiously switch interpretations of the very same texts, depending on whether the texts are about heaven or earth.

4. A Classless Society

Now that we have proposed our explanation concerning the kingdom, let us resume the thread of our argumentation in this chapter. The teachings of Christ upon which the first Christians were able to base their establishment of communism are, among others, Mark 10:25, Luke 6:20, 24, Matthew 6:24 (= Luke 16:13), and Luke 16:19–31. The first three refer to the kingdom, hence the above digression was necessary.

Of course, the first Christians were also influenced by Jesus' example and personal conduct. For Jesus, whether the conservatives like it or not, *was in fact a communist*—as can be seen in John 12:6, 13:29, and Luke 8:1–3. Judas "carried the purse," so they had everything in common and each received according to his need.

The doctrinal betrayal of later centuries, as we have seen, has sought to interpret this communism as a "way of perfection," not to be identified with the simple fact of being a Christian. But such an interpretation is dashed to smithereens when it impinges on the fact that Jesus made the renunciation of property a condition for simply "entering into the kingdom" (cf. Mark 10:21, 25). There is no room for a third way, when the dilemma is to enter into the kingdom or not to enter into the kingdom.

Besides, hypothetically, if being communist is more perfect than simply being Christian, I should like to know why they forbid it—why they teach that what according to Jesus is more perfect is evil. It is easy to see that the famous "way of perfection" is a mere escape route invented when the church became rich and began to constitute an essential part of the establishment. If it is decreed that communism is more perfect, the logical conclusion would have been to betake oneself to promote its realization in the world. Instead the conclusion has been to devote oneself to combating it, and to persecute to the death whoever promoted it. It is difficult to imagine anything that would demonstrate more clearly that the "way of perfection" doctrine is just an escape route, just a doctrinal subterfuge.

It was not only Jesus' example that taught communism to the first Christians; it was his word as well. Scientific exegesis recognizes that Mark 10:17–31, about the rich young man, is more reli-

able than its Matthean (Matt. 19:16–30) or Lucan (Luke 18:
18–30) transcriptions, which make obvious editorial changes. A
simple comparison shows that Matthew and Luke had the text of
Mark before them. And yet this is precisely where one can feel the
difficulties and conflicts faced by the first missionaries when they
wanted to proclaim to the world this authentic logion of Jesus: "It
is easier for a camel to pass through the eye of a needle than for a
rich person to enter the kingdom of God" (Mark 10:25). Since
Jesus had already said, "The kingdom of God has arrived" (Mark
1:15), the question is who can and who cannot form part of the
kingdom which Jesus Christ is founding on earth. And what Jesus
says is: The rich cannot.

In order to sidestep the conflict, but without betraying the
words of Christ, the first missionaries added: "For men it is impossible, but not for God; since to God everything is possible"
(Mark 10:27). They meant that by an act of God it is possible for a
rich person to enter the kingdom—*by ceasing to be rich, of
course*, since otherwise they *would* have been betraying the
authentic logion of Jesus (Mark 10:25). Any minimizing interpretation of Mark 10:27 is incompatible with Mark 10:25, and incompatible with the declaration at the source of the pericope
"Go, sell everything you have and give it to the poor" (Mark
10:21). If they come to us now and say that to enter into the
kingdom a rich person need neither go nor sell everything he has
nor give it to the poor, this is no longer interpretation but bold
out-and-out tergiversation.

Verses 21 and 25 could have been invented neither by the missionaries nor by the communities nor by the editor Mark, since
these verses raise insuperable difficulties for the proclamation of
the gospel. They are the authentic words of Jesus. Everything else
in the pericope is open to question.

Recall that the question is simply that of "entering the
kingdom," and that, as we saw in Section 3 above, the kingdom is
on earth. Jesus goes about recruiting people for the kingdom, and
says straight out: the rich cannot be part of it. People generally
forget that "rich" and "poor" are correlative terms. We say that
someone is rich in contrast with the rest of the population, or with
a majority of the population, which is not. As we shall see at the
beginning of our next chapter, Jesus is not against wealth in the
absolute sense of the word, but in the relative sense, in the mean-

ing of social contrast. When he says "Happy the poor, for yours is
the kingdom of God" (Luke 6:20), and adds "Woe to you the rich,
because you have received your comfort" (Luke 6:24), he is saying exactly the same thing as in Mark 10:25: the rich cannot enter
the kingdom. Only the poor can. (In passing, let us observe that
this demonstrates that, as the vast majority of exegetes maintain,
Luke 6:20 is the original version and Matthew 5:3 the later, since
Luke 6:20 says the same as Mark 10:25, whose authenticity no one
denies.) Now, what this teaching is saying, in concurrence with
Mark 10:25 and Luke 6:20, 24, is that in the kingdom there cannot
be social differences—that the kingdom, whether or not it pleases
the conservatives, is a classless society.

The anticommunist reaction has to abominate this, of course.
But it is worth repeating that they themselves, in their eschatologi-
cal conceptions, admit that according to the Bible there are no
social differences in the kingdom. The only thing they are missing
is the place, since if the kingdom is on earth they indignantly reject social equality. This is why we introduced our digression in
Section 3 above. What they admit for heaven is, according to the
gospel, on earth.

Marx did not invent the classless society. Except for the formulation, the idea is unequivocally in the most authentic and least
disputed logia (Mark 10:21, 25) of Jesus Christ.*

*The Matthean version of Mark 10:21 is recognizably later: "If you wish to be
perfect, go and sell what you have," etc. (Matt. 19:21). Here there is question of a
perfection which is indispensable for entry into the kingdom (cf. Matt. 19:24),
clearly superior to the morality of the Jews (cf. Matt. 19:18-20), but not excluding
any particular group of Christians, inasmuch as it is impossible to imagine a third
alternative between entering the kingdom and not entering the kingdom. The same
thing appears with the only other occurrence of the adjective "perfect" (Matt.
5:48). As the Catholic exegete Rudolf Schnackenburg recognizes, "perfection is
demanded of *all*" (*LTK* 3:1246—emphasis his). Catholic J. Blinzler, as well, says:
"The requirement of perfection is for all" (*LTK* 10:864). The alternative is not to
enter the kingdom: "If your justice were to be no greater than that of the scribes
and Pharisees, you would not enter the kingdom of the Heavens" (Matt. 5:20).
And the contrast in Matt. 5:46-48 is not with Christians of lesser perfection, but
with "publicans" (v. 46) and "pagans" (v. 47). What is not demanded of all Christians is celibacy (cf. Matt 19:10-12)—here there is a contrast between "not all have
room for this word" on the one hand, and "but those to whom it has been given"
on the other. It is the passage about eunuchs. There is no indication that one
alternative is more perfect than the other. As Schnackenburg well says, "Jesus is
only making an observation: 'There are those who. . . .' Doubtless his preaching
of the kingdom had fired up some of his followers in such a way that they felt
called to a virginal or celibate life" (*LTK* 3:1245).

CHAPTER TWO

WHY COMMUNISM?

When Jesus says, "Happy are the poor" and "Woe to you the rich," he is not talking about riches in the absolute sense. That is, he is not condemning the physical fact of having great material resources. There is not that kind of asceticism in Jesus that almost instinctively hates well-being and abundance, the kind that always goes hand-in-hand with extreme "other-worldliness." In John 12:7 Jesus not only readily permits, but actually defends the sinful woman's anointing him with an oil of nard worth three hundred denarii (v. 5), which John calls very valuable (v. 3) and Mark very costly (Mark 14:3). In the wedding feast at Cana (John 2:1–11), Jesus was pleased to contribute, in order to enhance the merrymaking of the whole company, six twenty-gallon jars of very fine wine (v. 10). Jesus has no horror of wealth, neither in itself nor in its use and enjoyment. And surely he had read that Abraham, the model of Old Testament faith, had been rich (Gen. 13:2). The wealth of the whole people is also lauded in Deuteronomy 28:1–14.

But as we were saying, "rich" and "poor" are correlative terms. When Christ says, "Happy the poor" and "Woe to you the rich," what he is attacking is that some are poor and others rich. If I may introduce a technical term, it is *differentiating*, or relative, wealth that he condemns. But this he does condemn, impla-

21

cably—so intransigently and unexceptionably that official Western theology is too traumatized to take a really close look at the condemnation for fear the whole meaning of the Bible may depend on it. And indeed the entire history of the West has been a falsification of Christianity simply because it has not dared to look in the face the inexorable reprobation to which the Bible subjects differentiating wealth. History has decided to turn its face away and believe that the "preferential option for the poor" is a question of tenderness and nice sentiments, when in reality it is a moral question in the strict sense.

One of the effects of this deviation is that even Christology has become a tissue of trivial and irrelevant theses. In order to be objective in reading the gospel one has to stop imagining Jesus as the sweet, conciliatory sort. He was a cutting man. Has there ever existed, in all of history, a more intransigent person than the one who turned to those who spontaneously wished to follow him and stopped them dead in their tracks with: First go and sell everything you have and give it to the poor and then come and follow me? This is a statement that can have been made only in a harsh, pugnacious tone—the tone of the man who, when he talks about money, calls it the "money of iniquity" (Luke 16:9, 11), the tone of the man who was capable of shouting out, "Scribes and pharisees, hypocrites!" seven times running (Matt. 23:13, 14, 15, 23, 25, 27, 29), the tone of the man who, speaking about the temple, comes right out and says, "Not a stone will be left upon a stone" (Mark 13:2). Jesus had the character of a hardened revolutionary. It is time we understood that.

1. The Illegitimacy of Wealth

But let us leave the Christologies to themselves and listen to Jesus' own words. Jesus condemns differentiating wealth. The parable of the rich man and the poor one (Luke 6:19–31) is perfectly consistent with Mark 10:25 and Luke 6:20, 24. Escapist exegesis thinks the rich man ended up in torment because he did not give alms to Lazarus. But the reason for his punishment is not a matter for conjectures. The parable itself makes it explicit: "Remember you received good things during your lifetime, and Lazarus on the contrary evil things" (Luke 16:25). What is punished is differentiating wealth, in its purest expression. The parable does not say, because you lived in abundance—which would have been to condemn wealth in the absolute sense. It says, because you lived in abundance and Lazarus in misery. What is punished, in torment, is that some are rich and others are poor.

At no turn is it insinuated that this rich man was a person of especially depraved habits, or that in order to enrich himself he had committed particular acts of extortion or fraud which other rich persons do not commit. The only thing said of him is that he was rich and lived as if he were rich: "There was a rich man, and he clothed himself in scarlet and linen, and daily dined splendidly" (Luke 16:19). And since this is nothing but the story of someone who was punished in torment, the only purpose the parable can have is to tell us why. It would be unforgivably negligent of Christ if, as the escapists would have it, he did not tell us why. But he does tell us why: because the man was rich. This is the very title of the parable: "There was a rich man."

Official exegesis cannot bear this message. Its instinctive revulsion goes beyond its strength and lucidity. But a complementary trauma is still in store for the official exegesis: Neither does the parable suggest that the poor man was especially virtuous. Here as throughout the Bible, the poor person's interior dispositions are of no importance. He is rewarded for the simple reason that he is poor: "It happened that the poor man died and was carried by the angels to the bosom of Abraham" (Luke 16:22). The total incompatibility of this criterion with the official conception of what Christianity is ought to have called the official conception into question from head to foot—without the uncritical supposition that there is anything in the official conception not open to discussion, even the conviction that Christianity is a religion. The sole reason for the condemnation of the rich man ("You received good things in your lifetime, and Lazarus, instead, bad things") is precisely the reason given in Luke 6:24: "Woe to you the rich; because you have received your comfort." The disjunction now is between being able to accept Jesus, and being faithful to a "Christianity" that sets up a fundamental obstacle to the understanding of the gospel. The theologians who question the authenticity of the curse of the rich in the Sermon on the Mount have not taken into account the fact that it says exactly the same thing as the authentic parable on the rich man and the poor one.

Before we proceed, let us notice that at the end of the parable Jesus says, by implication but with all clarity, that his condemnation of wealth is the teaching of the Old Testament ("Moses and the prophets"). The rich man asks that somebody go to warn his brothers on earth, "so that they may not come to this place of torment as well" (Luke 16:28). The answer is, "They have Moses and the prophets" (Luke 16:29); "if they do not listen to Moses and the prophets, they will not be convinced even if someone rises from the dead" (Luke 16:31). This means: Anyone who reads the Old Testament knows that (relative) wealth is immoral; if people are so blind that they do not understand this moral reprobation when they read it, they will not be convinced even if someone rises from the dead. Jesus would have to say the same thing today with regard to his own teachings in the New Testament.

Since the Old Testament condemnation of wealth is clear, it is not a matter for wonderment that Luke 1:53 places it on the lips of Jesus' mother. Let us now join this text to Mark 10:25, Luke 6:20, 24, and the parable. It says, "He filled the hungry with good things, and the rich he sent away with nothing." It does not say that he filled equally with good things the hungry and all the inhabitants of the land—which is what a simple communist would have to do after "tearing the rulers down from their thrones" (Luke 1:52). It says he will fill the poor with good things and will send the rich away without anything. The same principle is formulated in Psalm 34:11: "The rich will be left poor and hungry." No one can take the Bible seriously without concluding that according to it, the rich, for being rich, should be *punished*. Not to admit them into the kingdom when the whole point is to establish the kingdom, is clearly punishment. To commit them to torment, as the parable teaches, is punishment. To deprive them of all their goods and send them off with nothing is also punishment—for the simple crime of being rich.

I can hear a cry of total indignation: "But why?" The entire Bible is going to answer us, in its language, in the subsequent sections of this chapter. But in this section, let us try to explain the "why" in our modern language.

From the texts cited, it is inescapable that according to the Bible there is no legitimate fashion of acquiring differentiating wealth.

Unless this moral thesis of economics is supposed, the punishment of the rich *in quantum* rich will be altogether incomprehensible. All these texts imply that only by illicit means is it possible to reach a higher economic level than that of the majority of the population. It is evident that "illicit" does *not* mean: by transgressing the positive laws currently in force. The fact of legislation of nations authorizing means of acquiring wealth does not make these means to *be* licit, does not *make* these means licit. If there is anything of value in the Christian intellectual tradition it is that the criterion of good and evil does not depend on current laws or decrees or customs.

To be concrete, let us suppose that a big Mexican industrialist, a bread manufacturer, wishes to explain his position to us. He leads us to the top floor of the tallest building in his plant, and there, through a large window, shows us the vast expanse of his economic empire. "Look," he tells us, "from there, what is now Seventh Avenue, to Luis Vives Avenue (which I built), there used to be nothing. Just meadowland. Do you understand? Before I started all this there was nothing here. Now, after what I have done—and because of what I have done—there is a whole plaza of wealth here, the most prosperous firm in this city. Get it? Before I built this there was nothing. Now there is wealth. The only conclusion is that I did it. And so it's mine. Can I offer you something?"

You sure can. You can tell us what you mean by "There was nothing." There were at least three things in this country: raw materials, labor, and market. If you had lacked even one of those three things, not only would you not have been able to do anything, you would not even have been able to have the idea.

The magnate interrupts us. "But I bought everything at a just price! In other words, I acquired everything by contract, to which both parties freely agreed!"

This is precisely the weak point of your reasoning. This is where it falls apart. The only way you can acquire wealth is to buy cheap and sell dear. You have no right to suppose that society accepted your self-enrichment and that of your fellows of its own free will, knowing that it remained subjected to the will and the constraint of your capital. Let us take a closer look. The country folk who sold you their wheat had no other alternative. Either they accepted the price you felt like offering, or their harvest would rot and they would die of hunger. Of course they agreed to the various contracts offered them—and congratulated themselves on having found a buyer. But objectively you cannot speak of freedom of contract when the only alternative is hunger and misery.

This is not an appeal to emotion. We are not being sentimental about the suffering that goes on in the countryside. This is not rhetoric but rational argumentation. The moralists of the establishment have completely passed over this fact: when I am threatened with hunger and misery my acquiescence is not free. As far as a valid or invalid contract is concerned they might as well be threatening me with a pistol.

Next, the people who sell their labor, the workers, when confronted with the employment offer you made them, had as their only alternative unemployment, and the disasters of all kinds that go hand-in-hand with unemployment. In other words either they had to sign your contract regardless of its terms, or face hunger and family disaster along with their wives and their children. It is a grotesque joke to talk about a free work contract. Of course the workers held a fiesta when they got steady work in your firm; but in terms of strict morality it cannot be said that they freely agreed when the alternative was hunger.

Note that I speak in the categories of the most traditional moral philosophy. If the parties do not enter into the contract with freedom and cognizance of cause, the contract is invalid, and all its effects as well. Its effects are your wealth.

And as for the market, as for the consumer: no one ever asks us whether we agree with the price of a loaf of bread. We pay for it or abstain from it. Of course we are at liberty to eat cob-loaves or candy bars. But we are not asked if we agree with the price of the candy bar, either. Either we pay, or we abstain from eating it. Of course we can always eat tortillas. But we aren't asked if we freely accept the price of the tortilla, either. And we do have to eat one of the three things. This is not a matter for discussion; it is an organic necessity. Where is the liberty?

The wealth you boast of could, and can, be acquired only by millions of expressed or implied contracts: contracts of sale and purchase of the raw materials, contracts of sale and purchase of the labor, contracts of sale and purchase of the end product. The only possible source of wealth is to make off with the difference. Well, those contracts are invalid, because the consent of the weaker party was affected either by the violent constraint of circumstances, or by radical ignorance of what he or she was doing (an ignorance cultivated by the establishment by every ideological manner and means), or by both at once. The mechanism of constraint functions across the gamut of the social groups, as we have seen. But even conjointly, it is absurd to suppose that society even as a whole is willing to have a small group acquire, whether little by little or all of a sudden, the power that henceforth will permit it to impose its will on the whole of society. Or if it did give its consent, it is evident that it did not know what it was doing, that someone defrauded it by concealing from it the true significance of the facts. And fraud or ignorance suffices to invalidate a contract.

Perhaps our industrialist will object, "But I bought the raw materials and the labor at market value, and I sold my bread at market value at the price at which bread is sold in this part of the country."

I answer, in the first place this has absolutely nothing to do with the moral plane which is the basis of our discussion. The contracts were not signed by both parties freely. The price of the labor in the labor market is *imposed* on the worker, just as both of the other prices are imposed on the weaker party.

But in the second place (and here is where we touch the systemic nerve of the question—right here is where the medieval doctrine of the just price betrays its superficiality, and at the same time unmasks itself as part of the establishment), as we were saying, the market value is *imposed* on the weaker party. The market value must always be the one that allows merchants and managers to take a profit. This, according to the medieval doctrine, is the "just price"—the one that permits "each person to live according to his social position." Naturally, it is supposed that there ought to be various social positions. But the differentiating social position of the rich can exist only to the extent that they take a profit. In other words, when we suppose that there is a just price we are committing the fallacy of begging the question—by presupposing that there is a legitimate manner of acquiring differentiating wealth. This is precisely what the Bible denies. None of the means of acquisition can be legitimate, because the terms of the contract are necessarily *imposed* on the weaker party, which invalidates the contract together with all its effects.

The establishment ideologues, like the Chicago Boys and, earlier, the whole classical school of economics, have deliberately generated confusion as to who determines prices—so that the exploited may believe the prices determine themselves all on their own, or are determined by some kind of natural causes, somewhat as if they were determined by God and hence beyond appeal. But in a mercantile economy, the market price is necessarily the one which allows capital to take a profit. Otherwise capital is not invested. Hence it is the rich, and no one else, who determine the market price.

If there were true freedom and cognizance of cause, the workers would refuse to work unless they were guaranteed the same standard of living as that of their employers. And differentiating wealth would be done away with automatically.

Our mogul objects again. "But if there is going to be an exchange of merchandise, there has to be some just price."

I reply: Now that is just the point. What is in question is whether a system can legitimately exist whose resources and productive activity *are* intended for exchange—when it is possible to establish a system whose resources and productive activity are destined exclusively for the satisfaction of the needs of the population. The former system necessarily involves the forcible imposition on the weaker party to the contract of such a price as will permit the stronger party to acquire differentiating wealth. This is nothing but the systematic exploitation of some persons by others. The moralists of the establishment have passed over the fact that my contractual agreement is not free when I am threatened with hunger—because they consider this threat to be a natural one, simply the necessity we are all under to work for a living. But the necessity we are all under is to work for the satisfaction of needs, not to work to make some rich at the expense of everyone else so that they dominate everyone else. If the proletariat were not the victims of cultivated violence and ignorance, they would automatically refuse to work for the enrichment of a few. At the same moment the capitalist system would cease to exist.

Even within capitalism itself, it is a patent fallacy that entrepreneurs deserve profit on account of risks they take. The value of the product is exactly the same whether risks are taken or not. Thus the mere fact of taking risks does not create value in a product, does not add anything to it. In no way is it legitimate to remove a part of the product in order thereby to remunerate an activity which has contributed nothing to its value. But the real question is whether a system ought to exist in which anyone *has* to take risks, when we can produce exactly the same goods in a system without individual investment and without anyone's risk. To defend the former system you must either be masochistically in love of risk—or merely seeking a pretext for making differentiating wealth look honest. In actual fact it is uncritically *supposed* legitimate—and gets the post-factum message of either the "risk" sophistry or some other specious "justification."

The deep undercurrent, running along beneath the surface energies that are its corollary, is the fixed idea that differentiating wealth is an indisputable given. This is the mere historical continuation of the notion that some are born to be masters and others to be slaves, that some are born for a higher standard of living and others for a lower. This is why the Bible directly attacks differentiating wealth. Where a determinate kind of work is concerned, the first thing that has to be clarified is whether it is necessary or unnecessary. If it is unnecessary it should be eliminated. But if it is necessary, nothing and no one can legitimate the punishing of the one who performs it with a lower living standard.

Another empty pretext, like the risk pretext, is to say that the capitalist contributes to production by doing mental work. Actually, as Frank Cunningham says well, capitalists have no work to do at all, neither mental nor manual, if they so wish, for they can hire others to do it.

The greater part of their "mental work" contributes nothing to the effective production of the goods, but consists in thinking up ways to "kite" negotiables, ways to create artificial needs for the consumer, ways to squeeze more labor out of the work force, ways to carry on commerce more effectively, to drive out the competition, and the like. Or, in the case where their mental work does indeed contribute to production, this is but the contribution of one person among the many whose contribution and toil are necessary, in combination, to make a product. They should receive appropriate wages in remuneration, like the others.

As nothing justifies penalizing certain necessary types of labor with an inferior standard of living, it ought to be obvious that the alleged legitimacy of differentiating wealth is a mere historical prolongation of the slave mentality that says some are born to live better than others. This is indubitably how the authors of the Bible, and Jesus with them, perceived the affair. Hence their implacable condemnation of differentiating wealth. Why communism? Because any other system *consists* in the exploitation and spoliation of some people by others through the imposition of different prices. Just because of that.

2. The Spurious Origin of All Wealth

As we have seen, Mark 10:25, Luke 6:20, 24, 16:19–31, 1:53 necessarily imply that there can be no legitimate means of acquiring differentiating wealth, since there is no other explanation for the castigation of the rich for the sole fact of being rich. But according to Jesus the same condemnation of wealth as such is to be found in the Old Testament (cf. Luke 16:29, 31). We must look into this. The material is so obvious and abundant that it will show us the prodigies of tergiversation and voluntary blindness that the theologians and exegetes, and even the translators of the Bible, have had to deploy in order to muffle a book whose solitary intent was to change the world and eliminate injustice.

The evangelists borrow their terminology from the Greek translation of the Old Testament worked out in the second century B.C. by the legendary Seventy Translators—hence the name *Septuagint* ("seventy") Translation. In Greek, wealth is called *ploûtos*; a rich person is a *ploúsios*; and to grow rich is *ploutéo* or *ploutizo*. This group of words, this root, appears in the Septuagint some 180 times: seventy-six times it translates the Hebrew root *'ashar*, fourteen times the Hebrew root *hhaíl*, seven times *hamon*, six times *hon*; and the other occurrences are mistranslations, or are found in portions of the Old Testament which were not written in Hebrew.

Even the quantitative distribution of the occurrences of the root *plout-* is noteworthy: six times in the Pentateuch, nine times in the premonarchical historical books—very few occurrences. The barrage comes in the historical books of the monarchy, in the

Prophets, in the Psalms, and in the sapiential books. Hauck and Kasch give a pretty fair explanation: "In ancient Israel, as in Homer's world, there were famines (Gen. 41 ff.), but no social question" (*TWNT* 6:321). To put it more precisely: The historical fact is that in primitive Israel there were no social contrasts, that is, there was no differentiating wealth. This is why there is so little talk of wealth. Indeed it is even praised, for it is the wealth of the whole people—in Deuteronomy 28:1–14, for example. By contrast, the moment we set foot on the historical terrain of differentiating wealth, the condemnation of the rich as such is a central theme, without any loopholes, in the authentic Old Testament tradition—that is, until the era of the Hellenistic influence in the sapiential books.

A massive fact, which exegesis has not dared to take a close look at, is the identity between the "rich" (*'eshir*) and the "unjust" *(resha'),* the connection is so close that many times the sacred authors do not even have to say "the rich"—it is enough to say "the unjust."

We can document this identity by examining Isaiah 53:9. The first two stichs of this verse constitute a "synonymic parallelism" (typical of and very frequent in the Bible), and the last two make up another one.

> They placed his tomb with the unjust,
> and his sepulchre with the rich,
> although he committed no oppression
> and had no fraud in his mouth.

The reader readily perceives how natural the synonymity is in the mind of the author, how extreme is the degree of mutual implication obtaining between the rich and the unjust. The plain, unencumbered fact confronting Isaiah is that the servant of Yahweh has been buried in the cemetery of the rich, and not in the squalid potters' field where the poor buried their dead. This seems to Isaiah to be an indignity—because the servant had never committed either oppression or fraud, which, by definition, are characteristics of the rich. The synonymic parallelism consists in expressing the same idea twice, but in different words the second time from the first.

The escapist maneuver was initiated by the later editors of the

Hebrew Bible themselves. They could not modify the hard text, for they would have been accused of falsifying. But in a footnote they propose that the text is suspected of having been corrupted in the course of the centuries, and they try to get us to read *'osse ra'* instead of *'ashir*, which is what is in the text. Thus we would have "evil-doer" instead of "rich person," and the identity would be between the unjust and the evil-doers instead of between the unjust and the rich. It seems to have slipped the editors' minds that there are no special cemeteries for evil-doers. What does the reader think of the ingenuity the establishment must have had to employ in order to go on considering the Bible to be its sacred book without being continually set on its ear by encountering that the rich are condemned for the fact of being rich?

Claus Westermann's translation, in the influential ATD collection, also translates "evil-doers," and is rid of the problems. The Zurich Bible, which is the most popular German translation, also gives "evil-doers"—and does not even give an explanation. The New English Bible, which is the best English translation (Oxford and Cambridge), substitutes "a burial-place among the refuse of mankind" for "and his sepulchre with the rich"—and thus likewise effects the disappearance of the synonymity between rich and unjust. The Spanish translation of Nácar-Colunga, likewise, puts "evil-doers" where the text of Isaiah says "rich." Alonso and Mateos do the same. Bover-Cantera says "the corrupt" in place of "the rich." Cosmetic surgery at every turn. May I be permitted to take advantage of this opportunity to ask the reader not to trust published translations. In this book all biblical citations are translated directly from the original.

Many Old Testament commentators have dedicated hundreds of pages to the problem that exists for the sacred authors in the fact that the unjust (*resha'im*) are happy and enjoy prosperity and God does not intervene to punish them. But these theologians have focused the whole problem badly and have misunderstood it from the beginning, as we shall see in the early part of the following section. The sacred authors know that *all* differentiating wealth is ill-gotten, that it has necessarily been obtained by despoiling and oppressing the rest of the population, and that therefore to be rich is to be unjust. They sigh for Yahweh to intervene and reestablish justice by despoiling the despoilers. For the sacred authors, the problem of evil is a social problem.

But now we come to the central theme of the Old Testament. Let it not be thought that when Amos attacks "those who accumulate rapine and spoil in their mansions" (Amos 3:10) he is referring to certain rich persons in particular, determinate individuals who in order to enrich themselves have committed some special act of extortion or fraud which other rich persons do not commit. These fantasies have been theology's dishonest resort. The plain reality confronting Amos is the mansions and palaces of the rich of the city. That simple fact, and nothing else, is the target of Amos' invective. Neither does Isaiah 53:9 refer to the tombs of certain rich persons in particular. When Amos says "rapine and spoil," he is speaking of *all* differentiating wealth. He is defining wealth. There is not a single datum in the texts to justify the supposition that he is alluding to certain rich persons in particular, or to certain ways of acquiring wealth as contrasted with others. It is ludicrous for theology to attempt to reduce all these prophetic diatribes to the anecdotic—to "special circumstances." If there were any such special circumstances is it not perfectly obvious that the text would have clearly delineated them in order to justify the prophet's rage and fury? Here escapist theology's method pushes the limits of the unscientific. As if an author could appeal to special circumstances without being obliged to say what they were!

The same occurs with Jeremiah 6:6-7, where Jerusalem is described as follows.

> All is oppression in her midst.
> As a spring gushes with its waters,
> so does she gush with her evil.
> "Rapine, spoil!" is the cry within her,
> ceaselessly sorrow and hurt before me.

Neither in text nor context is there a single datum to permit us to conjecture that at the moment of this vehement denunciation there are any special violent acts of extortion being committed in the city, of a crueler quality than the ordinary. If there were, the Book of Jeremiah would have listed them—as in fact it always does when concerned with some particular incident, in order plausibly to introduce the crashing jeremiad of indignation. What the prophet sees in Jerusalem is merely the "normal" life of a city, in which the rich become richer and the poor continue in their misery. Jeremiah calls this oppression rapine and spoil.

The case is just the same with Habakkuk 1:3–4, where the prophet complains to God:

> Why do you make me look at iniquity,
> and I have to witness harrassment,
> and violent oppression and spoliation, before my eyes?
> Quarreling and wrangling spring up;
> for law is disappearing,
> and right never appears.
> The unjust man corners, traps the just one:
> plainly, this is a twisted rightness!

Once again, neither text nor context provides any basis for the attribution of this fusillade to any "special situation." What Habakkuk sees before him is the ordinary life of a city like Jerusalem. This ordinary functioning of the city the prophet calls "violent oppression and spoliation." What is really right, he says, never appears: the unjust person has the just person in a corner, and what appears is "twisted rightness," or distorted legality.

Plainly, this "twisted rightness" is the official legality of exploitation, the "free" contractual agreement the weak and impotent enter into because they have no other remedy. No one has managed plausibly to interpret the "cornering" to mean anything else. Hence, to declare that what is happening is that the unjust man is surrounding the just one with false witnesses and other lackeys (Karl Elliger) is to miss the whole broad point of the prophet's denunciation, and to leave verse 4 disconnected from the "spoliation" of verse 3. The "cornering" and false legality (the "twisted rightness") produce the spoliation as their effect. The efforts of the commentators are directed toward the discovery of some rare and special situation, while the broad intent of the text is evident from the words "and right never appears." It seeks to describe a situation that is constant.

What we have seen in the preceding texts is equally verified in Ezekiel 45:9 and Isaiah 59:7, 60:18: the rapine and spoliation denounced here likewise cannot, except by unbridled whim, be attributed to any peculiar situations or to some great and anonymous oppressors. When there are questions of particular incidents or persons, the prophetic books point these out. The Prophets have been read without the wish to understand them—with the desire instead that what is read not apply to the reader. This is why it comes to mind to guess at some very particular crime against which the prophet's volley is being discharged—without saying what it is.

Equally condemnatory of the ordinary life of a city, that is, of the ordinary enrichment of the rich, is Amos 5:7, 11, which refers to the same travesty of right and law which we have just seen in Habakkuk:

> . . . Who convert right into bitterness,
> and drag justice in the dust. . . .
> Therefore, because you trample down the poor man,
> and extort portions of his wheat—
> you build houses of ashlar
> but you shall not dwell in them,
> you have planted select vineyards
> but you shall not drink their wine.

Ashlar houses mean rich people's houses. The reason the rich can construct magnificent dwellings is that they trample the poor and gradually take the bread out of their mouths. Besides, if we observe what is said in Genesis 43:34, the noun *masse'et* should be translated in the dictionaries as "small portion," and not simply "portion." Amos analyzes, with perfect perspicacity, the source of differentiating wealth: it is accumulated by continuously depriving the poor of a small portion of their income. The rich have been able to erect their mansions precisely and solely by permanently sucking away at the quality of life of the poor. Naturally everything is done in perfect legality—hence Amos says they convert right, or law, into bitterness. In the section just above we saw that prices are imposed on the population in such a way as to insure that capital can obtain continuous profit—whether it is a question of the price of the raw material, or of the labor, or of the product sold to the consumer. We anticipated this analysis in the foregoing section for a reason: the prophets make the same analysis in different words. The diminutions of the wheat of the poor ("portions," v. 11) cannot be separated, however much routine exegesis may wish to do so, from the "right converted into bitterness" (v. 7): the spoliation operation is the legal, habitual one—the one carried out on a daily basis with the approval of law and custom.

It is signally impossible to anecdotize this verse of Amos. No one can think that the rich had armed servants making continual incursions upon the houses of the poor and divesting each person of only little portions of wheat—entirely apart from the fact that this would not be in conformity with, but in transgression of the law of the land. Hans Walter Wolff, the most prestigious of the commentators of Amos and Hosea, when he comes to the problem of "situating" Amos 5:1–17, simply admits defeat: "Of none of the statements of Amos in this section can it be said with precision where it was uttered" (*Biblischer Kommentar*, XIV/2:275). What is curious is that exegesis thinks it has to go in search of the particular, when it is the manifest intent of the prophet to describe and condemn a state of affairs that is general and constant.

There is not the least likelihood of truth in the exegesis which translates *masse'et* as "tribute" in this text, with the insidious intent of interpreting Amos' diatribe to be directed exclusively against rulers. The only two texts which the dictionaries can cite in favor of this translation (which would get the rich off the hook) are Ezekiel 20:40 and 2 Chronicles 24:6, 9; but both of these texts are concerned with portions brought to Yahweh in a sacred offering. This noun never denotes a civil tax. Accordingly, it is unscientific (and escapist) to translate it as "tribute."

The "little portions of his wheat" of Amos 5:11 can only consist in the underpayment of the workers, the short measure to the consumer through high prices, and the take of the big businessman, who buys the underpriced harvest which small farmers are able to sell only by refraining from consuming it. These are precisely the three avenues of the acquisition of wealth which our foregoing section singled out as dominated by the prices determined by the strong party to the contract. Any other interpretation of Amos 5:7, 11 would have to invent, for its own sake and without textual basis, a whole novel about armed attacks of the rich on the homes of the poor—incursions which would have the unprecedented characteristic of not sacking the reserves of wheat, but of delicately removing just a little portion.

And lest there occur to anyone the subterfuge of imagining that the rich of Jerusalem deserved Amos' barrage because they were particularly perverse in their methods of acquiring wealth, it is worth noting that Amos 5:7, 11 is pronounced against Sichem, or Samaria.

Micah 2:1-2, as well, is concerned with explaining the general origin of wealth. For this purpose it employs the verb *'ashaq*, which signifies, with complete precision, violently to seize what is another's, to oppress, to harass a weak person by snatching away what should be his or hers. (See this verb in Mal. 3:5; Ezek. 18:18, 22:29; Lev. 6:2-4, 19:13; 1 Sam. 12:3-4; Ps. 105:14; Jer. 7:6; Hos. 5:11, 12:8; Amos 4:1; Jer. 21:12; Ps. 72:4; and so on.) The verb strictly denotes exploitation. Micah 2:1-2 says,

> Woe to those who contrive iniquity,
> who scheme evil on their beds
> and carry it out at the crack of dawn
> because it is in the power of their hands.
> Fields they covet they snatch away,
> houses, they sweep away;
> they exploit the man and his house,
> the human being and his inheritance.

Unless we invent romances to detour the message to the anecdotic, the bare fact confronting Micah is the ordinary acquistion of wealth by some and the consequent impoverishment of the others. Consider this other condemnation, formulated in Isaiah 5:8:

> Woe to those who hoard up house on house,
> and link field to field
> till they occupy the whole place,
> and there they are alone in the middle of the land!

The actual, plain fact to which this reprobation refers is exactly the same as Micah was focusing on: the rich keep acquiring property. According to the prophets this fact can only be explained by the exploitation and violence perpetrated by the rich upon the rest of the population. Note that both of these texts immediately continue with the annihilating punishment sent by Yahweh (Mic.

2:3-4; Isa. 5:9-10). This means that both of these texts consider the simple acquision of wealth by the rich to be criminal. In both it is obvious that there is no question of methods of growing rich that are especially perverse, like the falsification of documents or the murder of legitimate proprietors. What is criminal is simply the accumulation of one house after another, the collection of one piece of land after another—that is, the acquisition of wealth (differentiating wealth, it must be remembered). Christ knew very well what he was saying in the answer the rich man received in the parable. The condemnation of the rich is clear in the prophets, and in the Old Testament in general. And notice the synonymic parallelism of Psalm 62:10:

> Confide not in exploitation,
> and make no illusions about spoliation;
> place not your heart in the wealth that grows great.

The wealth that grows great, or the acquisition of wealth, is synonymous with the spoliation and the exploitation. It is perfectly well known to the authors of the Old Testament that no one can acquire wealth without quietly despoiling and exploiting the rest of the population. It can only be owing to an immense toil of ideology and falsification that in the West a conviction which is so central and so evident for the Bible can have been buried and forgotten.

Jeremiah 5:27-28, too, tells us how the wealth of the rich originates.

> Like cages filled with birds,
> so are their houses full of what they have taken by fraud:
> this is how they have become great and rich.
> Fat and sleek they have grown;
> they went beyond words of evil:
> they did no justice, they trod upon the rights of orphans,
> they respected not the justice of the poor.

One cannot ask for anything more explicit. Wealth is acquired by defrauding the rest of the population, by trampling justice and the rights of the poor under foot. The only reality, the naked fact which Jeremiah has before him as he launches this invective, is the houses of the rich, the wealth of the rich. It is altogether clear that no other objective datum forms the occasion of these invectives. And we could quote a dozen more. It is perverse of the exegetes to prefer to "explain" them by the "innate rusticity" of these individuals called prophets, who could not bear the sight of abundance and luxury without exploding in insults. To refute this "explanation" all we need is to point out that the prophets specify the spoliation of the poor, fraud, and injustice as the only possible source of the wealth; hence their indignation is moral—pure indignation at injustice. It is strange that these exegetes call themselves Christians, when it is an established fact (see Section 1, above) that Christ made this prophetic condemnation of wealth his own.

The reason why these conscience-tranquillizing theologians have not felt themselves annihilated by these unequivocal prophetic condemnations is that they have invented the notion that they refer to some special group of rich persons, who have committed, in a determined moment and place, acts of fraud and outrage which are not the ordinary manner of acquiring wealth. The subterfuge is scientifically insupportable. It is as if the biblical condemnations of lechery and adultery could be nullified by postulating that they refer to certain particular individuals who have committed lecheries and adulteries that were especially perverse. It is as if the condemnation of murder alluded to certain historical homicides which were invested with special malice. If the resort of anecdotization is legitimate, if one can appeal to special circumstances without indicating what they are, then the Bible can teach us absolutely nothing. It turns into a strange book of vague anecdotes (since no one is willing to specify the concrete circumstances) in an unusual collection of historical curiosities—whose insertion into real history, moreover, has yet to be effectuated.

No, what Jeremiah had before his eyes when he pronounced the words we have cited was the "normal" spectacle of the wealth of the minority of the population in contrast with the situation of the majority. Of this wealth, as such, he asserts that it is acquired on the basis of systematic injustice and spoliation.

Why communism? Let us see whether anticommunists understand the reasons. Because any other system is strictly immoral.

Because any other system consists in the forcible and ceaseless spoliation of the majority by those who live on a superior level, convinced that the rest were born as inferior beings. Why are the rich punished for no other crime than that of being rich? Because the very fact that they do not perceive that they live on spoil is due to the contempt that prevents them from understanding that the work and toil of everyone else confers upon them too exactly the same right to live well. Because the rich are the historical heirs of the masters of a slave society, though the juridical formalities have changed. Why is Lazarus rewarded without any merits except being poor? Because creation, as it has historically developed, has penalized him without any particular guilt of his own. He did not ask to come into the world. It is the fault of the rich that his right to live well has been pitilessly ground into the dust by the wheel of creation which God set in motion. Theology has been a deceit—for not having dared to read the Prophets and Jesus Christ.

The numerous prophetical descriptions of wealth are, all of them, condemnatory. Not all of them explicitly assert (as the ones mentioned do, along with Mic. 3:9-11, Amos 2:6-8, etc.) that wealth is acquired by spoliation and fraud and injustice, but all of them condemn wealth. And this implies that they consider it ill gained, without exception and on principle. They have no need to investigate the rich person's biography in every case. They have no need to examine the history of the concrete fortune in question. They know that no differentiating wealth can be acquired without spoliation and fraud.

Certain establishment scripture scholars give the perverse insinuation of rusticity a twist that at first sight is more acceptable. They say that the prophets are simply longing for the simplicity of Israel's life in the desert when Yahweh delivered them from Egypt. At best this is an atrocious superficiality. The motive of the prophets is their clear understanding of the injustice committed by the rich. Their moral analysis is so explicit that to attempt to distract us with the notion of nostalgia is simply comical—especially since we know that the sojourn in the desert had taken place five or six centuries before and that none of the prophets, or grandfathers of the prophets, was there. The reason the prophets refer to the desert generations is that in those times there was no differentiating wealth among the people of Israel. What certain prophets are evoking is this: a society without social contrasts, without social classes.

In spite of their participation in this baseless intimation of nostalgia, Hauck and Kasch make the following objective observation on the prophets' critique of the class society. Their comment is valid in itself, and can serve to conclude our treatment of the prophets.

> But these repeated attacks of the Prophets on the upper class (Jer. 5:26–31; Ezek. 22:6–13; Amos 3:10, 5:7–12) are stereotyped, that is, *they are not directed against individuals but against the class as such.* This is also demonstrated by the predictions of calamity which they likewise direct, not against the individuals, but against the group (cf. Isa. 3:1ff., 3:16–4:1; Jer. 5:26–31; Ezek. 22:24–31; Amos 5:7–12; Mic. 2:1–11), and expressly include the rich. These will be cast into hell together with all the opulence and splendor of Jerusalem (Isa. 5:14); the wealth of the rich will vanish like dust (Isa. 29:5); the rich city will lie devastated and deserted (Isa. 32:12ff.); the women of the upper classes will be stripped of their social position (Isa. 32:9–12) [*TWNT* 6:322 (emphasis added)].

To have to call the prophetical reprobations stereotyped because they impugn the social class and not the individuals is a prejudice of Hauck and Kasch; and in the texts they cite there is nothing stereotypical. But the very fact that the condemnation of wealth in the Old Testament occasionally does become stereotyped indisputably demonstrates the Old Testament's conviction that differentiating wealth cannot be acquired by legitimate means.

3. The Problem of Evil: A Social Problem

The poor did not ask to come into the world. Their sufferings, deprivations, and humiliations are completely unmerited. Since it was God who set in motion the machinery of creation, God ought to feel a certain responsibility, even though it is the rich who are at fault for the injustice committed against the poor. "Never forget the life of *your* poor," the Psalmist tells Yahweh (74:19). It is this theology of responsibility for creation that the commentators forget when they devote so many pages to the problem of evil. The poor person has a right before Yahweh by the mere fact of being poor: "Hear me, Yahweh, and answer me *because* I am poor and needy" (Ps. 86:1).

Psalm 37, which these commentators consider perhaps the most typical of those concerned with the problem of evil, by no means treats only of the fact that the unjust (i.e., the rich) prosper. This is only half the problem. Just as much if not more emphasis is placed on the necessity that the poor take possession of the earth: "And the lowly shall become the lords of the earth" (v. 11), "the just shall inherit the earth" (v. 29), "he shall lift you up to take possession of the earth" (v. 34). It is astonishing that the commentators do not take into account that it is the poor who are speaking in the passages they cite. With their mentality, light years removed from an identification with the poor, naturally they have missed the whole thing. The problem is that the rich have seized the earth and are not permitting the rest of the population to live. But since, to these commentators, the mere mention of class struggle appears as an abomination, they have unscientifically decided to isolate the question as if it were chemically pure: the wicked prosper.

They forget that "wicked," or "unjust" (*resha'im*), is simply another designation for the rich, as is demonstrated in Isaiah 53:9, which we studied at the beginning of Section 2, above. Otherwise it would be quite a coincidence that it is precisely the unjust who prosper. Psalm 49, viewed by these commentators as another of the most typical psalms concerned with the problem of evil, does not say, "Fear not when the unjust grow rich," but it says:

> Fear not when *man* grows rich,
> when the opulence of his house waxes [Ps. 49:16].

The problem is not the one that exegesis has thought—that precisely the wicked or unjust grow rich (what a coincidence!)—but that any particular persons at all grow rich. These are called wicked or unjust precisely because they do grow rich, because, as everybody knows, all differentiating wealth is the fruit of injustice and spoliation. This is why the psalm says "Fear not when *man* grows rich."

Chapter 20 of Job, which according to these commentators competes with Psalm 37 in point of being typical, leaves no room for doubt as to what the wickedness of the wicked consists in:

> Because he oppressed the poor, and left them in the lurch,
> [therefore] he stole houses instead of building them.
>
> [Job 20:19]

It is the same description the prophets make of the wealth of the rich. Accordingly it is not that the wickedness of the wicked consists first in something else and afterwards that they grow rich into the bargain, but that their wickedness consists in their growing rich, since the acquisition of wealth is possible only by oppressing and exploiting the poor. And so the same chapter says

> Their children will have to make restitution to the poor,
> their hands will have to return their riches. . . .
> He returns his profit unswallowed,
> he enjoys not the fruit of his commerce [Job 20:10, 18].

If they must make restitution it is because they have robbed the poor. The problem is not simply that they acquire wealth, as if the wealth came out of nowhere. To the letter, verse 19 says what we have just transcribed: the rich did not build their houses; they stole them—by the method of oppressing and exploiting the poor and then abandoning them. Let us look again at Psalm 37, the one that is the most characteristic. Just as Psalm 49 does not say, "When the wicked grow rich," but "When *man* grows rich," so Psalm 37 does not say, "Do not be indignant when the unjust prosper," but "Do not be indignant against the *one who prospers*" (v. 7). And just as Job 20 explains the opulence of the rich by the oppression of the poor, so Psalm 37 relates the prosperity of some to the fact that they draw the sword "to cut down the poor and needy" (v. 14). No one who has read the prophets can doubt that these passages are simply descriptions of the rich—not of some wicked persons or other whose malice consists in some other thing.

Keep in mind that I am citing precisely those parts of the Bible that the commentators recognize as documents concerned with the problem of evil. Another is Chapter 24 of Job. And here we are astounded all over again. It is an implacable description of the exploitation suffered by the poor at the hands of the rich, and it even specifies the laborers who with their feet "press the wine, but themselves suffer thirst" (v. 11); "in the field they cut the master's fodder and harvest the vineyard of the unjust one" (v. 6); "they go naked, without clothing, and bear the sheaves while they starve" (v. 10). The complaint of this chapter is against those who "lead off the orphans' donkey and take the widow's ox in security" (v. 3), so that "all the poor of the earth go hide" (v. 4). The fact that exegesis has not seen that it is the rich who are being accused in *this* chapter is the last straw indeed. The description of the situation of the workmen includes no features that could arouse the suspicion that their employers are peculiarly wicked in any special sense of this word. What the poor are suffering is ordinary exploitation. And if this chapter, by the consensus of the exegetes, is characteristic of the problem of evil, then the problem of evil is simply the social problem in its purest expression. Otherwise it would be too much of a coincidence that none of these documents is able to speak of the "wicked" without mentioning the poor by contrast. Evidently the wicked are the rich.

Now let us broaden our crucial search for the identity of the *resha'im* by extending it throughout the Psalter, beyond the parts usually recognized as documents of the problem of evil. Inasmuch as the word *sadiqim* ("just [ones]") or its singular occurs fifty-two times in the Psalter, as against eighty-two occurrences of *resha'im* or its singular, in *Marx and the Bible* I proposed translating the latter by "the unjust," although in the present book I have used "unjust" and "wicked" indifferently. It can surely be said that the Psalter presents a struggle of the just against the unjust. But a good number of commentators (Weiser and Kraus, to name just two) and translations (e.g., the German of Zurich and the Dutch of Amsterdam) have found the trick of translating *resha'im* as "atheists"—an ingenious expedient for converting the struggle into a war against irreligion when it is actually a war against the rich. I am not saying that *resha'im* means "rich." It means "unjust." What I am saying is that the Bible calls the rich unjust.

The commentators and translators just mentioned base their choice, precariously, upon two passages. Psalm 10:4 places these words on the lips of the unjust: "By no means will he come to investigate; there is no God." And Psalm 14 (=53): v. 1, asserts: "The *nabal* [foolish person] says in his heart, 'There is no God.' "

The first thing we have to ask is why they do not translate *nabal* as "atheist" every time the word appears, while they do say "atheist" here when the word *resha'im* appears. But very well, these are peccadillos. In the second place, if lechers or murderers say there is no God, this is not sufficient grounds for asserting that the meaning of the word "lecher" is "atheist," or that the meaning of the word "murderer" is "atheist." This demonstrates that the translation mentioned is unfounded and tendentious.

But in the third place, if we are meticulous about it, the *resha'im* and *nabal* are not even atheists. In Psalm 10, which mentions the *resha'im* in verses 2, 3, 13, and 15, we read in verse 11: "He says in his heart, 'God has forgotten, he has his face covered, he can never see anything.' " In Psalm 73, which refers to the *resha'im* in verses 3 and 11, we find: "They say, 'How is God to know? Is there knowledge in the Most High?' " And in Zephaniah 1:12, " . . . Who say in their heart, 'Yahweh works neither good nor evil.' " In Psalm 94:7: "And they say, 'Yahweh does not see it, the God of Jacob does not realize.' " In Job 21:14: "They say to God, then: 'Go away from us, we have no wish to know your ways.' " As the reader sees, not only is there no documentary basis for translating *resha'im* by the word "atheists," but the documentary basis obliges one to assert that they are not atheists. They deny that God can see and punish their crimes, and they even address God. Psalm 14 (=53) refers to the *nabal* (foolish one). And as for Psalm 10, since the *resha'im* say in the same breath that there is no way he will come to investigate, one cannot read too much into the statement that there is no God. At most, one will have to assert that at times they are, or some of them are, atheists. But taking everything into account, the question is superfluous, since even if all the unjust were atheists this would not be the same as the word "unjust" meaning "atheist." There are no limits to the arbitrary methods utilized by the establishment in its escape from the Bible.

Let us proceed. Against two or three Psalmic texts thematizing the vertical relationship of the *resha'im* with God, any reader can cite two hundred describing these persons in their horizontal relationship with their neighbor. When the question arises how to translate the actual term, this is the fact which is decisive. Therefore to translate it too as "sinners" is totally unfounded and escapist. Of course they are sinners. But the fact that, for example, all torturers are sinners does not authorize us to say that the meaning of the word "torturer" is "sinner." There is a very precise word for "sinner" in the Bible: *hhote*, from the root *hhata*, "to sin."

The horizontal relationship just mentioned brings us back to our thesis that it is precisely the rich whom the Bible calls "unjust." When Psalm 14:4 says that the unjust "devour the people," and Proverbs 30:14 that they "gobble up the needy from the earth, and the poor from among humanity," since no one can think there is any question of cannibalism, who can it be who eat up the poor but the rich? See Micah 3:3 and Habakkuk 1:13. Unless we manage to imagine, without any foundation, some "special circumstances" or other, what the Psalmist has before him is the ordinary life of a city, or of a society, in which some are rich and others are poor. The "devouring" metaphor refers to the habitual exploitation of the poor by the rich. Thus it becomes clear whom the Psalter has in mind when it speaks of the unjust.

Likewise, when Psalm 35:10 says to Yahweh, "You who deliver the poor from the one stronger than he, the poor and the needy from the one who despoils them," who must be the one stronger than the poor? By definition, one who is not poor. Clearly, the Psalter divides society into two classes—the poor, and those who are stronger than the poor. This verse asserts that the latter class "despoils" the former. The identification of the unjust with the rich could not have been made more evident.

Attention should be paid to the fact that it is the *same* idea that is expressed in Psalm 82:4 as in Psalm 35:10, but in these words: "Deliver the poor and the needy, save them from the hand of the *resha'im*," and that this formulation recurs innumerable times in the Psalter. Society is divided into two classes: on one side are the poor, and on the other those who are stronger than the poor and are called *resha'im*. To fantasize special incidents is capricious and invalid. If the Psalter is focusing on the ordinary life of a society, the *resha'im* can be no one but the rich. I repeat, by definition: those stronger than the poor are those who are not poor.

Psalm 10:14-15 tells Yahweh, "The poor man abandons himself to you, you succor the orphan; break the arm of the unjust and wicked man." Since no one can think that the unjust are physically attacking the poor man and the orphan, as this would be to fall into the anecdotic, the passage must be begging Yahweh for protection from an aggression which is habitual against the poor. And this can only be the customary exploitation carried out by the rich.

The whole Psalter is concerned with aggression against the orphan (Ps. 10:14-15, 82:3-4, 94:3, 6, 146:9), and against the widow (94:3, 6, 146:9). If it is chimerical to romanticize personages and physical attacks, the Psalter must be speaking of the commercial speculator, or of the usurer, who after the death of a debtor who was the head of a family, exacts by the force of law (Habakkuk's "twisted rightness") payment of the debts which the deceased has not managed to discharge, and to this end seizes the goods which the widow and the orphan have inherited. Job 24:3 has already told us, "They lead off the orphan's donkey and take the widow's ox in security." No one has been able to explain in any other way the aggression that the Bible says widows and orphans suffer. Now, the speculator and the usurer are typically the rich of the locality. As it is the *resha'im* whom the Psalter accuses of this aggression, their identity becomes evident. Their injustice or wickedness does not consist in any special delict, but in the ordinary, "legitimate" exploitation by which the wealthy acquire wealth.

Still further, fraud and fakery are characteristics of the *resha'im* that are incessantly denounced in the Psalter, for example 5:7, 10:7, 24:4, 28:3, 35:20, 36:3-4, 40:4, 43:1, 50:19, 52:6-7, 55:23, 58:4, 62:4, 109:2. One is forced to infer that the oppression and spoliation which are also mentioned, with identical frequency, are not carried out by means of assault or armed incursion, but by means of cleverness and cunning—in other words, by a spoliation which is ordinary and legal. For example Psalm 55, referring expressly to the *resha'im* (v. 3), makes this denunciation: "Never are oppression and fraud missing from their marketplace" (v. 11)—evidently alluding to the manner in which the traders grow wealthy. This is called oppression for the reason set forth in Section 1 of the present chapter: the consumer population have no remedy but to respect the prices imposed by the rich. The identity of the *resha'im* is again abundantly verified.

All things considered, the Psalter is a combination of short literary compositions devoted to speaking against the *resha'im*; but there occur fifty-seven designations of the poor: twenty-three times *'ebion* ("needy"), five times *dal* ("indigent"), twenty-nine times *'ani* ("poor"). Is it not sufficiently eloquent that in order to talk about the "unjust" one has to refer to the poor fifty-seven times? Whom can the Psalms be talking about but the rich?

The ruin and final punishment of the *resha'im* is desired and announced time and time again by the Psalter. But notice how it is formulated in Psalm 52:5, 7–9: utter ruin will befall the one who "relied on his own great wealth and drew his strength from crime." The identity of the unjust becomes explicit. Here we have to repeat, with respect to the entire Psalter: the Psalmist's anguish does not well up when the *wicked* person becomes rich, but "Fear not when *man* waxes rich" (Ps. 49:17), "Do not become inflamed against *him who prospers*" (Ps. 37:7). The subject is the rich as such. The Psalter's other name for the rich is "the unjust."

4. Reprobation of Profit

From the viewpoint of the logical thread of this chapter, Section 3 has been an excursion, motivated by the fact that the so-called problem of evil has served exegesis as a pretext for distracting itself from the true message of the Bible, which is a tightly packed condemnation of wealth. Let us now resume the thread.

We saw that in the Old Testament, not only is differentiating wealth reproved but the reason for the reprobation is given. No differentiating wealth can be acquired without spoliation, fraud, and systematic violence. Now, from the viewpoint of economic theory this can be tacked down in more systematic fashion if we focus on the very concept of profit, since, as we set forth in Section 1, differentiating wealth can be gathered only by accumulating profit.

The overwhelming documentary datum is that the Bible condemns *all* profit. For corroboration, we might run the following test. Let the reader forget all we have said in this chapter. Let us begin afresh. The reproval of all profit suffices to condemn unequivocally all differentiating wealth, since the latter can be procured only by piling up profits. When communism is rejected today, it is done by cynically concealing and smothering the fact that the Bible condemns all profit without any exceptions, and that profit is the essence and mainstay of capitalism—that if profit were ever eliminated capitalism would disappear at the same moment. The reason why in capitalism goods are not produced for the satisfaction of necessities but for exchange is that they are produced for profit. As an answer to the question posed in the title of the present chapter, this fourth section would suffice.

The Hebrew word for profit is *besa'*. If we except one ironical use (Judg. 5:19), and four metaphorical uses (What do we "gain" by doing this or that?—Gen. 37:26, Mal. 3:14, Job 22:3, Ps. 30:9), every time the Bible speaks of profit it is in order to reprove it. There are nineteen passages, and the reader can verify them: Exod. 18:21; 1 Sam. 8:3; Isa. 33:15, 56:11, 57:17; Jer. 22:17, 51:13; Ezek. 22:13, 22:27, 33:31; Jer. 6:10, 13; Mic. 4:13; Hab. 2:9; Ps. 10:3, 119:36; Prov. 1:19, 15:27, 28:16. Here, however, I shall translate two of them because standard translations tend to cause confusion and render them unrecognizable. Proverbs 1:19: "This is the path of all who make profit: It will deprive of their life all who have committed it." And Proverbs 15:27: "The one who makes profit brings down his house in ruin." In the other seventeen passages I only remark that the original says "profit," "gain," and not "booty" or "theft of goods" or "unjust gain," as the establishment translations trickily put it, so that the obvious condemnation does not fall on the head of profit as such. As the translators are convinced that profit is licit ("God could not have permitted his church to fail to condemn it," as if God cannot permit evil, which is the same as to suppose that evil does not exist), they instinctively adulterate the text and put some other word where the text says "profit," since it is the transparent intention of the sacred author to condemn it.

The etymology of *besa'* ("profit, gain") is incision, extraction by cutting with a knife. But the conspiracy of the ideologues of the establishment has reached the degree that it manages to keep the truth even from readers who have taken the trouble to study

Hebrew. The dictionaries of biblical Hebrew translate *besa'* as "unjust profit"—and then forget to add that the Bible has no word for "just profit"! That is because for the Bible there is no such *thing* as just profit. It is as if when we came to the word *na'af* ("adultery") we were told it means "illicit adultery." Establishment botching knows no bounds.

The biblical condemnation of all profit is a round one and without loopholes. And as we were saying, the whole puzzle falls together in a dazzling concurrence of elements. The Bible not only reproves the result, which is wealth, but concentrates as well upon the process by means of which the result is attained—and reproves the process in the same way.

The condemnation of differentiating wealth is the most solid and inescapable documentary datum in the Bible. This is why Jesus of Nazareth calls money the "money of iniquity" (Luke 16:9,11), adopting the expression of the Jewish Book of Henoch 63:10, which is a faithful continuation of the Old Testament tradition. Saint Jerome comments, "And wisely he said 'with unjust money,' for all riches derive from injustice, and unless one loses the other cannot gain. Therefore it is clear to me that the familiar proverb is eminently true: 'The rich is either unjust, or heir of one unjust' " (*PL* 22:984). It should not be thought that we are inventing a new interpretation of the Bible here. Before the church associated itself for all future centuries with the exploiters, all the fathers of the church understood the Bible as we have.

To confirm this, very briefly and in passing, we might take note of a literary fact which theology is at pains to pass over, and which confirms what we have just said. As can be seen from Tobit 4:7 ("Turn not your gaze from anyone poor"), Tobit 4:10 ("Alms indeed preserve one from death") and Tobit 12:9, "Alms indeed preserve one from death," late Judaism arrived at the notion that giving money to the poor preserves a person from death. But the brutal fact that theology refuses to look at is that the original Hebrew Bible calls that act of giving money to the poor not "almsgiving," but "justice" *(sedaqah)*.

Proverbs 10:2: "Justice delivers from death." Psalm 112:9: "With generosity he gives to the poor, his justice abides for ever." Tobit 14:11: "Behold what almsgiving does, and what it is that justice preserves from." This is a fundamental datum, and is taken up in Matthew 6:1–4: "Be careful not to practice your justice before men, in order to be seen by them. . . . Therefore when you give alms do not send the trumpeters before you. . . . Instead, when you give alms. . . ." Clearly, the act which we think of as an act of almsgiving is, according to the Bible, an act of justice—restitution of what has been stolen. This is why Jesus calls money the money of injustice or iniquity.

And hence it is that Augustine says, "To succor the needy is justice" (*PL* 52:1046). And Ambrose, "You are not giving the poor person the gift of a part of what is yours; you are returning to him something of what is his" (*PL* 14:747). Chrysostom: "Do not say, 'I am spending what is mine, I am enjoying what is mine.' It is not actually yours, it is someone else's" (*PG* 61:86). Basil: "It is the hungry one's bread you keep, the naked one's covering you have locked in your closet, the barefoot one's footwear putrifying in your power, the needy one's money that you have buried" (*PG* 31:277).

That the holy fathers are serious about this may be seen from Jerome's phrase quoted above: "All riches derive from injustice." The fathers understood very well the reiterated analysis made by the Bible and studied in our present chapter: All differentiating wealth is acquired by exploiting and despoiling the rest of the population. Hence they see almsgiving as restitution in strict justice.

This biblical analysis, as we were saying, is conclusively corroborated by the condemnation of profit, since the process which issues in wealth is the ongoing accumulation of profit. But there is more. The Bible itself examines separately the various ways by which profit can be obtained and reprobates them all. But before sketching this condemnation it may be well for us to answer an objection about profit-taking in general, which is really just foolishness but which the establishment is unable to refrain from raising. We will be told that Jesus does not adopt the Old Testament condemnation of profit, for in the parable of the talents (Matt. 25:14–30, Luke 19:11–27) the Lord says to the bad servant, "You ought to have deposited my money with the bankers, and so at my return I would have recovered my own with interest" (Matt. 25:27) and charges his servants with the task of doing business with the money he places in the hands of each.

The objection ignores the most elementary thing: that this is a parable, a comparison. Any modern commentator, even the most conservative, points out that the elements of the real life situation that are the terms of comparison are no more than a literary vehicle for the real lesson the parable seeks to teach. Here the lesson is that we are obliged to contribute the talents of our human capacities for the realization of the kingdom. And that is all. The fact that a parable *compares* something with an element of real life in no way means that it *approves* this element.

Or consider this parable: "If the lord of the house knew at what hour of night the thief was going to come, he would be on watch and would not permit his house to be broken into. Therefore you also be prepared, for at the moment you least think, the Son of Man will come" (Matt. 24:43–44). Jesus compares himself to a housebreaker. Why do our objectors not draw the conclusion that it is licit to devote oneself to the profession of a thief, a housebreaker?

And in the parable of the steward expressly called unjust (Luke 16:1–8), who swindled and committed embezzlement in full consciousness and deliberation (vv. 6, 7), why do they not conclude that the career of a swindler is legitimate and commendable?

But the last straw is, that in the *same parable* on which they think they can base their objection, if they were logical they would have to draw the conclusion that he was a fine person who, with unbridled covetousness, "withdraws what he did not deposit and reaps what he did not sow" (Luke 19:21, 22), or who like the oriental despot Archelaus, takes vengeance on his adversaries and amuses himself by watching them have their throats cut (Luke 19:27).

Only a desperate theology could have taken the fact that Jesus, in composing a literary comparison with profit-taking, does not expressly caution that the elements of his comparison constitute illicit conduct—and manufactured out of it an approval of profit! And as he also fails to do so in the matter of the housebreaker and the on-stage throat-slitting. The parable as a literary device would lie in total havoc if these cautions had to be issued at every turn. It is not worth the trouble to delay any longer on an objection which is a pure case of *ignoratio elenchi*, or arguing beside the point. When I exclaim, "This delay is torture!" no normal person will take it into his or her head that I am pronouncing upon the morality or immorality of torture. If someone says "This news is an atom bomb," no one in his or her right mind will conclude that the speaker is in favor of manufacturing atom bombs.

We have noted that the Bible does not rest content with simply reproving profit-taking in general. It itemizes its reproof. Profit can be made through any of these three channels: commerce, loans at interest, and productive activity itself (the process of production). And the Bible condemns the profit made through each of the three. Let us examine them in order.

> For the sake of profit, many have sinned;
> the one who tries to grow rich, turns away his gaze.
> Stuck tight between two stones,
> between sale and purchase, sin is wedged [Ecclus. 27:1–2].

It could not be more clearly expressed that it is illegitimate to obtain profit through the process that constitutes commerce: retaining the difference between the purchase price and the selling price. To boot, the same passage states explicitly that this profit-taking is the process which issues in the acquisition of wealth. Profit, then, is considered to be the source of (differentiating) wealth. We must add the present passage to the nineteen we listed at the beginning of this section which use the word "profit" (always to condemn it). Not all of the original Hebrew of the Book of Ecclesiasticus has survived, but there is no doubt that here the original word was *besa'*. The only thing that is special is that this passage, while using the general term "profit," narrows its reproof to the gain that emerges between the buying price and the selling price. The text is in Greek.

Let us note in passing that in the verse immediately preceding (26:29) the Septuagint stylistically uses the adverb *mólis* ("hardly, with difficulty"), which cannot be an exact translation of the original because there exists no word corresponding to it in Hebrew. If we turn to Proverbs 11:31, where *mólis* is also used, we see that it translates the original *hen*, which means "lo and behold." Based on the synonymic parallelism with the second hemistich, it is certain that Ecclesiasticus 26:29a means, "The trader does not deliver himself from sin"—which is surely what the Septuagint means, although it makes use of a more polished expression.

Now let us look at the second channel of profit—interest on loans. The Hebrew word for "interest" is *neshek*. Its root means "to bite." Without a solitary exception, each time the Bible uses *neshek* it is to condemn it. There are twelve occurrences: Exodus 22:24; Leviticus 25:36, 37; Deuteronomy 23:19 (thrice); Ezekiel 18:8, 13, 17, 22:12; Psalms 15:5; Proverbs 28:8. But note that a loan can mean not only a money loan, but the loan of a thing as well. Accordingly, the absolute biblical prohibition of interest-taking embraces also what we today call collecting rent, or hire. See Deuteronomy 23:19: "You shall not lend to your brother at interest, neither at interest on money, nor at interest on aliments, nor at interest on any other thing which produces interest." Leviticus has the same thing. Perhaps we ought to have said that profit is taken through four channels; but as it is the same texts that forbid interest and rent, our catalogue has been under three rubrics.

As we see, the Bible condemns every kind of interest, high or low. Translating the word *neshek* as "usury" suited an escapist intent—as if only very high interest were forbidden. Besides, the word "usury" does not fit where the interest collected is on things and not money. Surely what the Bible forbids is usury—but always remember that there is no such thing as nonusurious interest. There is another word—*tarbit* (etymologically, "increase"), which occurs as a synonym with *neshek* in the texts cited (except in the ones from Deuteronomy and Psalms)—but it is equally condemned. We would have to translate it "revenue."

The third channel is the profit obtained in the very process of production. It must be kept in account that until very recent centuries the main productive activity was agriculture. In our Section 3 we have already seen the description given of the field hands in Job 24. But James 5:1–6 is more explicit in condemning the acquisition of wealth by the agricultural entrepreneurs. In order to understand the latter pericope we must note that James, as exegesis generally recognizes, impugns all the rich, not only those who are such by having defrauded workers.

The invective starts right in the beginning of the letter (1: 10–11) and is directed against the rich as such. See also 2:6, "Is it not the rich who oppress you and who hail you before the tribunals?" In our pericope itself we read, "You have lived on the earth in pleasures and luxuries, you have fattened your heart for the day of slaughter" (5:5). It is the simple crime of being rich—exactly as in the prophets and the Sermon on the Mount (Luke 6:24, "Because you have received your comfort"), and the parable of the rich man and the poor one (Luke 16:19). Consequently, the writer has no concern to characterize those he vituperates by something which other rich persons have not done when he tells them, "See, what you have whittled away from the pay of the workers who reap your fields cries out, and the anguish of the harvesters has come to the ears of the Lord of Armies" (James 5:4). What this verse is doing is explaining the origin of wealth. Its intention is not to refer to *some* particularly perverse rich people who have committed knaveries which other rich people do not commit. The letter's attack is against *all* the rich. The verse cited reinforces this attack by exposing the nature of the origin of wealth. The "whittling away" referred to is by system, not by special transgression committed by certain of the rich. To be sure, it is the rich who hail the poor before the tribunals (2:6). The law is on their side. It is not as if they whittled away the laborers' income illegally. The exploitation is systematic—"legal," as we observed in Section 2 of this chapter. For James, differentiating wealth can be acquired only by means of expropriation of the produce of the workers' labor. Therefore, following Jesus Christ and the Old Testament, James condemns differentiating wealth without vacillation or compromise. Profit made in the very process of production is thus specifically imprecated.

The biblical reprobation of differentiating wealth is cohesive and without loopholes. The attack is not only against wealth already acquired and established, but also on the sole means by which this wealth came to be, which is the taking of profit; and it is not only against profit in general, but also on the various kinds of profit—each and every one of the methods that can exist for acquiring profit in an economic system. With what conscience before God the theologians have been able to evade this absolutely central message of the Bible is beyond my comprehension. If we want to know "Why communism?" the response is unequivocal: because any other system *consists* in the exploitation of some persons by others. Just because of that.

Against this monolithic coherence of the genuine biblical tradition (including Jesus), the four or five texts of merely human prudence (which not for nothing are all found in the sapiential books) emerge as irrelevant. No sincere Christian can dissimulate the fact that the sapiential writings are the unreflected juxtaposition of biblical thought and extrabiblical, principally Hellenistic, thought. For instance consider this text of Wisdom 8:19–20: "I was a lad of good nature, and endowed with a good soul; or rather, as I was good I entered an unsullied body." Here, quite Platonically, the pre-existence of the soul is asserted—a doctrine irreconcilable with God's creation of the whole person as taught by the genuine biblical tradition (cf. Gen. 1:27, 2:7). The reader of the sapiential books must always be careful to discern what comes from the genuine biblical tradition and what comes from outside.

CHAPTER THREE

POLITICS AND
VIOLENCE
IN JESUS OF
NAZARETH

The endorsement of communism—and above all of its reason for being, which is the intrinsic immorality of relative wealth and profit—is right in the Bible. And it is in the Bible in a fashion so unconcealable and cutting that the only logical thing for the establishment to do would be to shelve the Bible among the books of antiquities and cease to consider it a sacred book of normative character.

The establishment has not done so. Every self-respecting civilization needs its sacred book. What the ideologues of the establishment have done for centuries and centuries is to latch on to three verses which (if they are not examined) seem to map out an avenue of escape and cling to them as if the rest of the gospel and the whole Bible did not exist. They are (in the official reading):

you will always have the poor with you; give to Caesar what is Caesar's; my kingdom is not of this world.

If these texts had not been available the theologians would have found another—any other, since the end is determined beforehand, namely, to avoid the message of Jesus, and to this end any means is good. There is no effort at all to place these texts in their proper context, nor to understand them according to the mind of the one who pronounced them, nor even, heaven help us, to determine the grammar of the texts themselves. It is terror— fear that we revolutionaries are right—that makes them snatch at three verses, disconnect them from everything else, and erect them into the sole criterion of good and evil. In their twisted understanding of these three texts, they conjure up the preposterous thesis that Christianity should not engage in politics—which does not prevent their engaging in politics, and on a grand scale, but independently of and contrary to the gospel—although they imagine that it cannot be contrary to it because they have already posited that the gospel has no political dimension.

It is obvious that if the present chapter seeks to ascertain the political dimension of the gospel it will have to occupy itself with these three texts one by one. In a fourth section we shall address the problem positively. And in a fifth we shall touch on the theme of violence.

1. You Will Always Have the Poor With You?

In his description of the communism of the first Christians, Luke notes expressly:

> There was no poor person among them, for whoever possessed fields or houses sold them, bore the proceeds of the sale and placed them at the feet of the apostles, and a distribution was made to each one according to his necessity [Acts 4:34–35].

This is "why communism": so that there may be no poor person among us. Recall that "rich" and "poor" are correlative terms. Luke is very conscious of the teaching of Jesus and of the prophets: that a society in which there are rich and poor is intrinsically immoral, since it implies perforce the latter's exploitation by the former. Unlike Jamblichus and Plato, Luke has an obligatory *moral reason* for communism. The fact that original communism failed does not mitigate the fact that its intention was to replace a society in which there are rich and poor. Establishment exegesis, along with its translations, ought to have noticed that at least the first Christians believed we would not always have poor people with us.

In the first place, the text to which so much allusion is made does not actually say "always," nor "you will have," as the most exact modern exegetes have already noticed. Eduard Schweizer does not say *immer* ("always") but *allezeit* ("all the time"). Walter Grundmann says *jederzeit* ("at each moment"). Vincent Taylor expressly notes, "The statement is not intended to assert that poverty is a permanent social factor (cf. Deut. 15:11) but is the background to *emè dè ou pántote échete.*" And as for the verb, it must have required an extreme case of blindness ever to have translated it in the future tense, for the original says "you have," and indeed twice in the same verse. This is how it should be translated:

> The poor you have with you at all moments [or "continuously"], and you can do them good when you wish; on the other hand you do not have me at all moments [Mark 14:7].

None of the manuscripts or variant readings ever dared to put "you will have" (*éxete*) instead of "you have" (*échete*). But what the copyists never managed to say even by mistake, Western translations have long dared, radically adulterating the text. The reader can still verify this falsification today in the Bible of Jerusalem, in French as well as in Spanish (not, however, in English). The rightist conviction that we are never going to change the world, and that there will always be poor and rich, cause the translations to ride roughshod over even the grammar.

And in the second place, the adverb *pántote*, which has customarily been translated "always," but which means "at all moments, continuously, habitually, at each moment, ceaselessly," is never used in the gospels with a verb in the future tense. It occurs thirteen times: Luke 15:31, 18:1; John 6:34, 7:6, 8:29, 11:42, 12:8

(twice), 18:20; Matt. 26:11 (twice), and Mark 14:7 (twice). In every instance it modifies a verb in the present or past tense. The idea is clear: for example, "to pray without ceasing" (Luke 18:1; the same in Rom. 1:10 and many times in Paul) does not mean that prayer continues for all future time, but that we do not cease to pray in the present time. When the gospels wish to say that an action or a situation lasts into the future without ever stopping, the expression they use is *eis tòn aiôna* (or else *eis toùs aiônas*). There are seventeen occurrences: Matt. 21:19; Mark 3:29, 11:14; Luke 1:33, 55; John 4:14; 6:51, 58, 8:35 (twice), 8:51, 52, 10:28, 11:26, 12:34, 13:8, 14:16.

As a result, to translate *pántote* as "always" in Mark 14:7 favored misunderstanding in the first place, since the idea is that the disciples will no longer be with Jesus continuously, as they were accustomed, because he is going to his death, but they could continuously bestow charity on the poor. A certain lapse of time is implied, but it is of present time. Still, the observation I want to make is that the rightists understood the "always" as "forever" simply because they were pleased to do so, since the adverb "always" does not necessarily mean that—neither in English nor in German nor in Italian nor in French nor in Spanish nor in Portuguese nor in Dutch. Hence to translate *pántote* in Mark 14:7 as "always" was not in itself incorrect. What was incorrect was the anxiety of the rightists to understand it to mean that class society would never be eliminated.

Let us examine a few parallel cases. I recall an Italian film, *Sedotta e Abbandonata*. In the courtroom scene, while the judge (the *Pretore*) is questioning the defendant and the witnesses, he addresses the clerk from time to time, "Lei scriva sempre, Signor Cancelliere"—literally, "Always write, Mr. Recorder," in the sense of "Keep writing, Mr. Recorder." Can anyone in his or her right mind understand that directive as if the recorder now had to sit there and write for ever and ever? It is the same in French: I may telephone a friend who I fear is no longer there and ask, "Tu es toujours là?"—meaning literally, "You are always there?" in the sense of "Are you still there?" No one could think that this "always" refers to the future. In all the languages mentioned above we find the same usage. "Durante toda la semana Elena ha siempre estado haciendo chistes," or "Helen has always been joking this week." There is not the faintest suggestion of the future—still less of all future time.

Now let us look at the gospel itself: "Son, you are always [*pántote*] with me and everything mine is yours, but we had to feast and celebrate because this brother of yours was dead and has returned to life, was lost and we have found him" (Luke 15:31–32). The "always" means: you are with me habitually. Not the most foolish reader understands this as: you and I shall be together for ever and ever. Then why did people take it into their heads to understand Mark 14:7 to mean: you will have the poor for ever and ever? See also John 18:20: "I always taught in the synagogue and in the temple, where all the Jews gather. Why do you ask me?" One ought to ask the rightists why they do not understand that Christ will keep teaching in the synagogue till judgment day.

Let us not tarry longer on this Gibraltar of an establishment objection—which goes up in smoke on the slightest contact with grammar. It would have sufficed to translate the verb as present tense ("you have"), as it actually is in the text, to watch the whole rightist war machine collapse in slapstick.

2. What Is Caesar's

The reader need not find it strange that these renowned objections turn out so flimsy and insubstantial. Their prestige over so many centuries never had a thing to do with the content of the texts. It came exclusively out of the preconceived attitudes of those who brandished them. That is why, when they are examined, nothing is left of them. In other discussions it sometimes happens that the outcome is indecisive, that some data are pro and some contra and it is a complex affair to strike a balance. But not with these glorious objections. They are false and the case is closed. Their reputation came not from the texts, but from the prejudice with which the texts were read.

The second objection is the one about "what is Caesar's":

He says to them, "Whose effigy is this, and inscription?"
    They told him, "Caesar's."
    And Jesus told them, "What is Caesar's, give back to Caesar, and what is God's to God" [Mark 12:16–17].

Let us note in passing that "deliver" or "give" are not precise translations of the verb *apódote*. In the Gospels, where it occurs twenty-seven times, *apodídomi* always contains the notion of giving back, returning, restoring. There is mischief afoot here. Just by translating literally, scholars could long since have put themselves on the alert.

As to this second rightist war-horse I have to say that scholars clarified the matter many years ago. I only want to call attention to what has been known for some time.

For what I am about to say, we should note beforehand that Albert Schweitzer, the only exegete to have been awarded the Nobel Prize, and Martin Dibelius, founder of the exegetical method called *Formgeschichte*, are generally recognized as two of the greatest New Testament exegetes of all times. And Guenther Bornkamm, for his part, figures among the most notable New Testament exegetes of this century; his book *Jesus von Nazareth*, a meticulous monograph of no easy reading, was printed in 75,000 copies between 1956 and 1965. Now each of these three authors is above suspicion not only of being socialist, but of being any kind of revolutionary at all.

Having made this introduction in order to qualify the objectivity of their thesis, I transcribe this paragraph from Bornkamm concerning Mark 12:17:

> From the point of view of form this logion is certainly constructed according to the so-called parallelism of members. But no one can seriously doubt that it is an "ironic parallelism" (A. Schweitzer, M. Dibelius). That is, the question about the imperial tax, which his adversaries thought such a dramatic one and posed so captiously, Jesus sidesteps [*Jesus von Nazareth*, p. 112].

To put it in other terms: According to the most detached and the least suspect scripture scholars of our century, *the marvelous statement about giving to Caesar is ironic*. Bornkamm also cites, in note 31, biblical scholars Eltester, Cairns, Sayers, Claudius, Wehrung, Luetgert, and Repgow. Be it carefully noted that we are not inventing an ad hoc interpretation that the statement is ironic in order to justify our revolutionary intentions. We are taking this interpretation from the hands of the most serious scientific exegesis, authorized by, and itself belonging to, the establishment. And we are taking it with the emphasis which that exegesis itself gives it: no one can seriously doubt that the phrase is ironic.

Here I could leave off my treatment of this second conservative war-horse. But I want to add how astonished I am that the irony in Mark 12:17 has not long since been seen. The setting is Jerusalem. It is a matter of historical record that the people of Jerusalem were strongly sympathetic to the Zealots—so much so that a few days later they demanded the freedom of Barabbas (Matt. 27:21, Luke 23:18, John 18:40). So the people definitely rejected the idea of recognizing Roman authority. The evangelists expressly call our attention to the fact that the question Jesus must answer has been posed for the purpose of "snaring him in his words" (Mark 12:13, Luke 20:20, Matt. 22:15). It was a trap. If Jesus denied the tax should be paid, he would be accused before the governor (Luke 20:20). If he admitted the tax should be paid, he would be recognizing Roman authority and thus fall from the good graces of the people. But rightist exegesis blunders into the interpretation of Jesus' reply as a recognition of Roman authority. So Jesus fell into the second alternative which had been set to trap him! Luke explicitly informs us that "they could not trap him in any statement before the people" (Luke 20:26), but rightist exegesis says he recognized the Roman authority, which was precisely the way to alienate the people.

Let us look again. The evangelists (Mark 12:17, Matt. 22:22, Luke 20:20) formally establish that Jesus' reply caused general admiration. It was brilliant, adroit. Will the conservative theologians kindly tell us what was remarkable about the reply if it was a recognition of Roman authority? The only intelligent way to handle the reply was to elude both snares at once, and routine exegesis has Jesus step right into one of them. How could his response have been any worse, since it was logically impossible to fall into both parts of the trap at the same time? If I may be pardoned the expression, at this point routine exegesis exhibits an obtuseness rarely seen.

The only escape was an ironical phrase which would neither recognize authority nor be accused of denying the obligation to pay the tax. Instead, we find attributed to Jesus' reply the only stupid option open to him.

However, let us go deeper, for this glorious objection actually turns back, boomerang fashion, on its authors. But note that logically speaking, the foregoing argument is independent of the following. The foregoing argument did no more than annihilate the objection: Jesus' reply cannot be interpreted as recognition of authority. The observations which follow demonstrate that his reply was actually an attack against authority.

Before the incident in question, Jesus had already proclaimed: "No one can serve two lords, for either he will hate the one and love the other, or he will cling to the one and scorn the other. You cannot serve God and money" (Matt. 6:24; cf. Luke 16:13). A person who has taught this in such categorical fashion cannot get out of it afterwards by saying you have to recognize and fulfill your obligation to the emperor and God at the same time. When he says "You cannot serve God and money" the whole force is in the "and." Pro-government theology all affirms that "and." The teaching of Jesus militantly denies that "and."

The most important datum for the interpretation of the statement about Caesar is that the civil authority, at this moment, is incarnated in a coin which Jesus asks to be shown. This, Bornkamm and his colleagues have not well considered. The statement "You cannot serve God and money" (Matt. 6:24) used the Aramaic verb 'abad, which means "serve" as well as "adore"; and this is the origin of our usage of "divine service" or "liturgical service" to designate acts of worship in Western languages. In the Old Testament, this is the verb (it is equivalent in Hebrew) repeatedly used to oppose the service and adoration of Yahweh to the service and adoration of the false gods (see for example Deut. 6:13, 7:16, 10:20). But whereas in the rest of the Bible and the Judaic literature the false gods are identified as demons (e.g., Deut. 32:17; Ps. 106:37, 96:5; Bar. 4:7; 1 Cor. 10:20, 21) or as "nothings" (e.g., Lev. 19:4; 1 Chron. 16:26; Hab. 2:18; Jer. 14:22, 16:19)—here, for the first time in history, on the lips of Jesus, the false god and rival of Yahweh which dominates society is something perfectly real and tangible: money. Western theology has failed to grasp that this (Matt. 6:24) is one of Jesus' most original teachings—perhaps the most original. Surely the most virulent. The real rival of Yahweh is money.

A gentleman who says we cannot serve God *and* money is shown a coin. And he exclaims, "Return to Caesar what is

Caesar's!'' Exegesis has not grasped the fact that at that moment the coin is the incarnation of all civil authority. The irony is not only patent, but terribly sarcastic. It is as if a Giovanni Papini, after having said that money is devil crap, had added: Give the money back to the government—and give God what is God's. When Bornkamm cautions against a revolutionary interpretation, it is because he has not understood Jesus' statement to the hilt. Jesus' ploy is to deny all governmental authority, but in such terms that no one can accuse him before the governor.

3. The Kingdom Is Not of This World?

Perhaps the most celebrated objection, the one which has marched in the most parades of triumph, is the third: my kingdom is not of this world. And yet it is the frailest and most chimerical of all. All you need to watch it float away forever is a Greek dictionary. The only problem is that our Western languages, with the exception of English, do not have the exact resources to translate John 18:36 faithfully word for word. It can be translated correctly only by adding to the number of words, or by substituting, for the original verb, another verb which makes it possible to retain the precise meaning of the preposition which follows the verb in the original. The original reads, *he basileía he emè ouk éstin ek toû kósmou toútou.* The whole meaning depends upon the preposition *ek.* And any Greek dictionary can tell you that *ek* signifies origin, place from which something comes, provenance, point of departure of something moving. Therefore in English it can be translated rigorously, thus: my kingdom is not from this world. In Spanish, as we have no unambiguous equivalent for the Greek preposition *ek*, we have to substitute *provenir,* "come forth," for the verb *ser,* "to be." Mi Reino no proviene de este mundo: my kingdom does not come forth from this world.

And that is all there is. Jesus never said his kingdom is not of this world. It is so simple, that it is unthinkable that this text can have been appealed to in good faith for centuries in order to place the kingdom in another world when the exact opposite is explicitly taught by all the other texts of Old and New Testament (see our Chapter 1, Section 3), including the Lord's Prayer, which these theologians and hierarchs pray every day.

Having the Latin preposition *ex* available, which faithfully renders the Greek preposition *ek*, the Vulgate did not do well to translate "Regnum meum non est de hoc mundo," since this laid the basis for confusion: *de* can indeed signify origin, but it can also signify pertinence, belonging. And yet the Vulgate itself sufficed to scatter its own confusion, since it goes on: "Si *ex* hoc mundo esset regnum meum. . . ." What happened was that the establishment had a vested interest in the matter, and snatched up the first phrase, dislocating it from even its most immediate context and brandishing it as proof that the kingdom of God does not call into question the kingdoms and social systems of this world. Let us not believe that these theologians were pining and sighing for that other world. No, they were afraid that the poor ("of such is the kingdom of God," Luke 6:20) would fight them for *this* world.

The precipitancy and desperation with which the theologians of the establishment have snatched up the first phrase has kept them from even reading the rest of the verse—in which Jesus repeats his thesis in other words: *he basileía he emè ouk éstin enteúthen.* In English this translates quite literally: "My kingdom is not from here." In Latin, the Vulgate translates perfectly: "Regnum meum non est hinc." In Spanish we have to use a circumlocution: "Mi reino no es oriundo de aquí, no se origina aquí"—my kingdom does not arise hence, does not originate here.

The Greek adverb *enteúthen* (equivalent to the Latin *hinc*) is altogether unambiguous. It designates the "here," but as locus of origin, as place whence something goes out, the point of departure whence something begins its movement. In the whole Bible, including the Septuagint Old Testament, this Greek adverb is used thirty-eight times. Only once does it have a figurative sense (the logical "hence it was that . . ." in 1 Esd. 4:22). Nine times it is found in idiomatic repetition, *enteúthen kaienteúthen,* meaning "from hence some and from hence others," that is, some on one side and others on the other: Exod. 17:12; Num. 11:31, 22:24; Josh. 8:22; 2 Sam. 2:13; Ezek. 40:49; Dan. 12:5; John 19:18; Rev. 22:2. The other twenty-eight times it is the pure "from hence" (or "coming out of here"): Gen. 37:17, 42:15, 50:25; Exod. 11:1, 13:3, 19, 32:7, 33:1, 5; Deut. 9:12; Josh. (A) 4:3; Judg. 6:18, 7:9 (A); Ruth 2:8; 1 Kings 17:3; Neh. (B) 1:1; Tob. (S) 7:11, 8:20, 10:10; Jer. 2:37, 45(38):10; 2 Macc. 2:32; Luke 4:9, 13:31; John

2:16, 7:3, 14:31, 18:36. The reader can verify this, keeping in mind that dictionary authors have no more data at their disposal than we have. Not one single time does *enteúthen* signify belonging-here. It always signifies origin, place from which something departs and comes forth. The fact that Jesus repeats his thesis employing this adverb instead of the substantive "world" is double confirmation that the idea is that of origin, of procession. The indubitable meaning of the preposition *ek* in the first clause of John 18:36 would have amply sufficed; but as if this were not enough, the adverb *enteúthen* at the end of the verse makes it airtight. What has happened is that the establishment has not had the remotest intention of verifying what it is that Christ said.

Saint Augustine understood the text perfectly: "Non ait: nunc autem regnum meum non est hic, sed non est hinc" ("He does not say, 'Now my kingdom is not here,' but 'is not from here' ")—*In Johannem Tractatus*, 115, 2.

The reader can see how the three big aces of the reaction turn out to be just three stacked decks. And the reader can see that in order to understand the real meaning of these three verses it was not necessary to wait for modern exegesis to get around to clarifying them, but there were evident and compelling elements in the text itself that should have been enough to make the escapists discard their interpretation without a trace. The false "interpretation" has been intentional. In the first and third texts the distortion was not even on the interpretative level, but on the perfectly obvious grammatical one. The falsification perpetrated by the official conception of Christianity has been deliberate. In particular, to teach authoritatively that there will always be poor people, and this as if it had been a logion of Jesus, implies a refined and unpardonable cruelty.

4. Jesus Engaged in Politics

Let us return for a moment to the end of our first chapter. A kingdom of God in which social classes are eliminated (Mark 10:25; Luke 6:20, 24), a kingdom of God which seeks to "tear down the rulers from their thrones and lift up the lowly, to fill the hungering with good things and send the rich off with nothing" (Luke 1:52–53), not only implies, but is, a political transformation of the broadest reach. Where by all that is holy do they get the thesis that Christianity should not engage in politics? To uphold an apoliticism of the gospel is to uphold the nonrealization of the gospel.

It is evident that it was the persecutions of the first three centuries, unleashed by the lords of this world, which constrained Christians to present a version of Christianity which would no longer provoke repression. But afterwards there was more than adequate time to lay aside this understandably opportunist and false version which interposes itself between our eyes and the texts, for the texts can be objectively analyzed. In the fourth century the church dispatched the kingdom to the other world, assuring the lords of this one that they could rest easily as far as the gospel was concerned. When the persecution was over, when the official church had acquired not only status, but dominant status in a class society, fear of repression ceased to be the motive for this documentarily indefensible falsification of the gospel. Now it was upheld for the personal convenience of the hierarchies, and for fear of a gospel which would unequivocally criticize the recently invented hierarchical structure of the church ("And call no one of you on the earth 'Father,' for your father is one only: the heavenly one"—Matt. 23:9). What is certain is that, first out of a fear of repression, and afterwards out of a fear of revolution, a conception of Christianity continued to be taught and dogmatized which, from every viewpoint, is irreconcilable with the texts.

The texts fairly shout their message. One had to go to real extremes to invent the notion that the Bible is not the only font of revelation, but that there is another font, which we were invited to call "Tradition." But the tradition of the holy fathers turned out to be as subversive as the Bible (see our Chapter 2, Section 4). And so it came about that this wonderful second font came to consist, for all practical effects, in the will of the reigning pope.

The whole theological process is sociologically understandable, but it has two sensational weak points.

In the first place, it is a logical blind alley. The authority of the church can only be demonstrated from the Bible; but then the Bible must have authority of itself, and have no need of the renowned second font in order to have this authority. Otherwise the demonstration of the authority of the church would be a rudimentary vicious circle.

And in the second place, the second font, if it is the font of one and the same divine revelation as the first, is useless if the texts of the first font are left intact. The inventors of the above theological synthesis have not changed the texts. The resulting doctrinal construct is unstable and explosive, because the biblical texts remain intact. And today we have the situation in which the official teaching is the precise contrary of what the texts demonstrate. The explosion is inevitable.

As we have stated, the thesis that the message of Jesus does not get involved in politics is simply outrageous. This thesis implies a complete misunderstanding of the prophets and a complete misunderstanding of Christ's intransigeant condemnation of the rich. The struggle for a society in which there will be no rich or poor is not a "preferential option for the poor," as Medellín and Puebla so inadequately put it. It is not an option, it is an obligation. Medellín and Puebla give the impression that it was some arbitrary decision of God or the Bible, which could be omitted without imputation of culpability. To the extent that one does not participate in this revolutionary struggle, one participates in the benefits of a society which lives essentially by exploiting and oppressing the poor. Merely abstaining from the struggle constitutes aiding and abetting the criminal act, and therefore constitutes complicity. The situation of the poor is injustice in the most strict, and commutative, sense of the word (see Chapter 2), in the sense that obliges to restitution. Even God is under obligation in this matter, for it is God who set in motion the machinery of creation which has resulted in tearing to bits the strict rights of the poor, who did not ask to come into the world in the first place.

The thesis that Christ did not engage in politics is a denial of precisely those historical facts which we know with the greatest certitude. I refer not only to the testimony of Suetonius, who, in his *Vita Claudii* (25:4) describes the Christians as "impulsore Chresto assidue tumultuantes" ("ever in frantic tumult at the instigation of someone called Chrest"), although this document would suffice. No, the most incontrovertible of all scientifically certain historical facts is that Jesus died by crucifixion and that crucifixion was the death reserved for political transgressors. No serious researcher omits this, but we shall cite only two. Johannes Schneider, in the article on the word *staurós* in *Theologisches Wörterbuch zum Neuen Testament* (8:573), says:

In the Roman provinces the punishment of crucifixion was one of the most powerful means for the conservation of order and security. The governors inflicted the death of the cross, proper to slaves, especially upon the freedom fighters who strove to gain their peoples' independence from the Roman authority.

As for a Catholic scholar, let us consult Heinrich Schlier: "The death of Jesus on the cross . . . is the death which the Roman authority inflicted on 'rebels and bandits' " (*Die Zeit der Kirche*, p. 59).

For more confirmation: the sign that Pilate ordered attached to the head of the cross of Jesus (*INRI*) specifies political delict as the motive of the punishment of this particular crucified criminal. Raymond E. Brown, a Catholic, comments: "All the Gospels agree that the charge of being a royal pretender was inscribed against Jesus" (*The Gospel According to John,* 2:919). Further, as Schlier observes, "from the words of Jesus about his kingdom Pilate could only infer that he was a king, and that accordingly his action concerned the political sphere. And what is remarkable is that Jesus admits it: 'You have said it' " (*Die Zeit der Kirche*, p. 63). Jesus was executed for political sedition. This is a fact that no serious person, Catholic, Protestant, or agnostic, can call into question.

Moreover, Matthew and Mark inform us that Jesus was crucified between two "robbers" (Matt. 27:38, Mark 15:27). Now, this was the depreciatory denomination applied by the authorities to rebels and insurgents, as can be seen by comparing "Barabbas was a robber" (John 18:40) with "who had been incarcerated for an uprising and homicide occurring in the city" (Luke 23:19). Consequently, Jesus was crucified side by side with two other rebels—only, he was more deserving than they, so he was put in between them, with a placard stating his crime: that of being a royal pretender.

No single historical fact about Jesus of Nazareth is more demonstrable than this one: that he engaged in revolutionary political activity. In his study on the parables (*The Jesus of the Parables*, p. 17), C.W.F. Smith comments very aptly, "No one would crucify a teacher who told pleasant stories to enforce a prudential morality."

Luke recounts an incident by which we can clearly see that Jesus had difficulties not only with the governor of Judea, but also, and earlier, with the ruler of Galilee, who was Herod Antipas.

Certain Pharisees appeared on that occasion telling him, "Go out and leave this place, for Herod seeks to kill you." And he told them, "You go and tell that fox, 'See, I cast out demons and work cures today, and tomorrow, and I go on the next day'—for it is unfitting for a prophet to die outside Jerusalem" [Luke 13:31-33].

Three things are evident in this little pericope. First, the absolute lack of respect with which Jesus speaks of the ruler. This is the language of a rebel, not of an obedient subject. Second, that Jesus himself realized that his activity and teaching were of a kind that would bring upon him the death penalty. And third, that not only the government of Judea sought to kill Jesus, but that of Galilee as well—which is understandable only if both saw in him a political danger. Herod's reaction is confirmation in advance that Pilate would be making no mistake. The popular movement that Jesus was stirring up had an evidently revolutionary character.

The evangelists pass over certain things in silence, of course. And this is understandable. Their editorial plan is to present Jesus as a martyr, murdered against all reason and justice. But in spite of the selective method that guides them, data filter through to the effect that, in the only two regions in which Christ carried out his activity, the government tried to kill him (successfully, in the second). This can only be because the revolutionary character of Jesus' proclamations constitutes a historical fact too massive to hide.

And let it be noted that the other Jewish leaders realized this fact as well. Once a certain moment had arrived in the development of Jesus' activity, they made this analysis: "If we let him continue this way everyone will believe in him, and the Romans will come and destroy our place and our nation" (John 11:48). There was no reason to fear that Jesus' movement would appear evil to the Romans unless it involved a threat to the government in power. I repeat the observation of C.W.F. Smith: No one would crucify a teacher who told pleasant stories to enforce prudential morality. I do not see how subtleties can overcome the data we have cited. The assertion that the gospel does not engage in politics is one of the most unreal and unrealistic theses ever formulated.

But we must examine the subversive character of Jesus' message more deeply. How could his message be apolitical if "the kingdom of God" means that God reigns and not human beings?

Granted, Pilate was a Roman. But it must be carefully kept in account that the ruler of Galilee was not a Roman but a Jew. What disturbed the Zealots was that the *Romans* ruled Israel. Jesus went far beyond the Zealots. Jesus left all nationalism completely out of his plans. (Hence the Jewish people finally abandoned him and went to the Zealots.) When Luke sums up the kingdom with "he tore the rulers from their thrones" (Luke 1:52), it is not just a question of Roman rulers, it is a question of every class of rulers. Jesus was incomparably more faithful to genuine biblical tradition than all the other Jewish revolutionaries of his time. God and human beings cannot reign at the same time.

This is what the oldest biblical tradition teaches. See Judges 8:22–23:

> And the Israelites said to Gideon, "You rule over us, you and your son and your grandson, for you have freed us from the hand of Midian." But Gideon told them, "I shall not rule over you, and my son will not rule over you, but Yahweh will rule over you."

The Bible expressly notes that when the monarchy was founded in Israel it was done against the will of God:

> Samuel was displeased by the word which they had spoken, "Give us a king so that he may judge us." And Samuel prayed to Yahweh. And Yahweh told Samuel, "Pay attention to the people in all that they tell you, for they have not rejected you, they have rejected me, that I may not reign over them" [1 Sam. 8:6–7].

New Testament exegesis cannot legitimately suppose that Jesus would lack the intelligence to discern in the Bible the most authentic and oldest teaching of God concerning government. It is enough to read the books of the Old Testament in the order of compilation to know that these two paragraphs (the one from Judges and the other from Samuel) are the first thing the Bible teaches about government. But we have the explicit words of Jesus besides: "No one can serve two lords, because either he will hate the one and love the other, or he will cling to the one and scorn the other" (Matt. 6:24). What is so strange, then, if when Christ proclaims that "the kingdom *of God* has come" (Mark 1:15), we recognize his message as the most subversive ever proclaimed in politics? Luke, in the text from the Magnificat just cited, interprets with perfect fidelity the revolutionary meaning of the gospel of Christ.

From the systematic viewpoint, it is to be noted that this radical anarchism (not anarchy) is quite coherent with what we have seen in the preceding chapters. Where there is no differentiating wealth, where economic activity is directly for the purpose of the satisfaction of needs and not for trade or the operations of buying and selling for profit, government becomes unnecessary. By no means is this the invention of Marx and Engels, as can be seen from the biblical texts we have cited.

5. Jesus and Violence

Finally, let us take up the matter of violence—for it is surprising, to say the least, that in spite of the fact that the more traditional moral tractates and the current chairs of moral theology teach the right of legitimate defense by the use of violence, the official versions of Christianity deny this right solely to the proletariat attacked on the scale of genocide.

And I refer not only to aggression committed by the police and the army, the aggression already being perpetrated in Latin America, which satisfies the doctrinal condition that aggression must precede a legitimate defense (a condition which itself is unjust); I refer principally to the aggression committed by the capitalistic system itself, which is far more evil. Millions of children die in the world each year from simple malnutrition. And many more are mentally deficient all their lives from the same cause. And many millions of human beings have their lifetimes cut in half from the same cause.

Now, it is not as if the resources presently existing in the world were inadequate to produce sufficient nutrition for all. Technologically it is possible. What is happening is that capitalism as a system does not permit existing resources to be directed to the satisfaction of needs, because the purpose it imposes upon them is the augmentation of capital. Unless a demand of buying power is foreseen which makes a profit likely there is no production; but the world's most tragic and urgent needs are without buying power and consequently cannot translate into demand. Capitalism has seized the resources of humanity, and physically kills millions of human beings day by day with hunger, or leaves them lifelong mental defectives. Would it be more violent to shoot them than to prevent them from eating? Where did this definition of violence come from? The aggression is right here, right now, in the form of genocide, and it is constant. By what prodigies of doctrinal immorality are its victims denied the right of legitimate defense? How can anyone think that it is less aggressive systematically to reduce the life and vitality of a human being than to cut it off suddenly?

The Bible teaches,

> Who spills man's blood,
> by man will his blood be spilled,
> for God made man to his image [Gen. 9:6].

It does not say that his blood will be spilled precisely by the hand of authority. It says: by another man. And in the series of instances in which the Mosaic legislation prescribes the death penalty (e.g., Exod. 21:12, 15, 16, 17), it is by a stoning to be carried out by the whole people (Lev. 24:14, 23, 20:2, 27; Exod. 17:4; and so on). This is violence; and it is not only permitted, it is commanded, by the one true God. The human community has to defend itself from its attackers. Now, the crime of killing millions of human beings by hunger, which is being committed at the moment at which you are reading these lines, is immensely more serious than those listed in the Mosaic law. Exodus 21:17, cited above, reads, "He who curses his father or his mother shall die without quarter."

Perversions of the gospel maintain that Jesus, by his divine authority, abrogated the Old Testament. With that the perverters feel authorized to write off Yahweh of Hosts himself, who so many times *describes himself* on the attack, "with hand aloft and flexed arm" against the oppressors (Deut. 4:34, 5:15, 7:19, 26:8; Exod. 6:6; cf. Ps. 136:12). And they pretend that all this violence is attributable to an imperfection, which according to them "still plagued Old Testament religion."

But in the first place, Yahweh, after all, is still the one true God, is this not certain? In the second place, the fact is that Jesus never disapproved his Father's conduct. And in the third place—and this is the *coup de grâce*, since theological discussions have altogether overlooked this datum—according to Mark 7:9–13 and Matthew 15:3–6 Jesus quoted the above-cited Exodus 21:17 right down to the letter, and not only approved it but defended it against the lax and sugar-coated interpretations of the scribes and Pharisees. In this verse is all the violence of the Old Testament, in all its splendor.

> It is nice how you can set aside God's command so you can hold on to your tradition. For Moses said, "Honor your father and your mother," and "Who curses his father or his mother shall die without quarter." Instead, you say . . . [Mark 7:9–11].

Jesus explicitly approves the use of violence. Note that in order to defend honor paid to one's parents against the compromising interpretations of the scribes and Pharisees, Jesus could have simply cited "Honor your father and your mother" from Exodus 20:12. But no, he draws on a different chapter of Exodus, and adds: "And who curses his father or his mother shall die without mercy." We have already pointed out that these executions were carried out by the entire people. Here we have sure documentary evidence, which no pedantry will manage to escape. Jesus explicitly approves and defends the use of violence.

It is dogmatic theology, not Jesus, which has decreed, by and of itself, that the characteristic of Christianity is nonviolence and nonvindictive justice. All the vindictive justice of the Old Testament is approved and defended by Jesus in this passage, citing Exodus 21:17. The characteristic of the gospel is the realization of the kingdom, in contrast with the perpetual procrastination of the kingdom. "Love your neighbor as yourself" (Mark 12:31) was already in Leviticus 19:18, and neither in the Old Testament nor in the gospel was this commandment understood to be at variance with vindictive justice and with the obligation violently to repel the aggressor of the human community.

The fact that Jesus maintains and defends Exodus 21:17 would be enough to demonstrate that the honey-sweet, saccharine gospel forged by establishment theology is counterfeit. Since the words we have cited are authentic logia of Jesus, it is evident that in his mind love of enemy (Matt. 5:44) is not at variance with repulsion of the oppressor, even by violence. Of course, as Comblin has said, the best demonstration of love for the rich is to divest them of what prevents their entry into the kingdom (cf. Mark 10:21, 25). But apart from this, what has happened is that a candy theology has grabbed "love your enemies" and torn it away from the whole gospel—and refuses to take the trouble to verify in what sense Jesus understood it. Evidently he does not understand it in a sense that would be incompatible with the obligation to repulse the aggressor of the human community by use of violence. The sense in which he understands it can be clarified later. But the sense in which he does *not* understand it is clear from the start. The sense in which he does *not* understand it is the one single sense which the ideologues read in "love your enemies." The procedure is dumbfounding. There is no least desire to verify what Jesus thinks. The only goal is to defend the status quo and prevent the revolution. So they think it is possible to "tear down the rulers from their thrones" by peaceful means?

The reaction adduces Matthew 26:52, "All who take up the sword, by the sword will die," a well-known adage ("who kills by steel dies by steel"). But they deliberately forget Luke 22:36, "Whoever has no sword, let him sell his tunic and buy one." They also purposely forget Matthew 10:34: "I came not to bring peace, but the sword." They pass over the fact that Matthew 23 is a page full of *verbal violence* unique in all literature of all time. And most of all they pass over the fact that according to John 2:14–22, Matthew 21:12–13, Mark 11:15–17, and Luke 19:45–46, *Jesus used physical violence* to drive the traders from the temple.

Let us suppose that, as the representatives of the establishment are accustomed tacitly to assume, there is a contradiction between Matthew 26:52 and the other two texts about the sword and the physical expulsion of the merchants. With what right do they simply abide by Matthew 26:52 and decree the other texts out of existence? With what apriorism do they decide that Matthew 26:52 is Jesus' authentic doctrine and the others are doctrinal or practical errors? Numerically the texts about the sword are two against one. With what right do they impose the obligation of *preferring* that one against the other two? Really it is Jesus' conduct itself which ought to be the norm of our understanding of his verbal pronouncements, and Jesus actually used physical violence. "Who takes up steel dies by steel" is what is known as an "occasional" statement: Jesus considered it useless—and it was useless—to offer resistance *in those particular circumstances*, and in order to deter Peter he quoted a well-known aphorism. Luke 22:36, as well as Matthew 10:34 (which is surely an expression originating with Jesus) are much more intentionally doctrinal, and much less circumstantial, than that aphorism.

It is criminal to defend repression by the procedure of quoting to the oppressed the verse about "turning the other cheek" (Matt. 5:39). The supporters of official theology will have to be punished for discouraging the struggle against injustice with this verse. By the grace of God I will practice the heroism of presenting the other cheek when *I myself* have been struck on the first. But this is a personal and individual matter. *What Jesus never said is: If they strike your neighbor on one cheek, turn your neighbor's other cheek*. And the proletariat are defending the bread of their wives and children, and the lives of all their comrades. Furthermore, according to John 18:22-23 Jesus did not present the other cheek when they struck him on the first. He protested with all his might. And who knows what he might have done if his hands had not been bound (cf. John 18:12). With what right does the church demand precisely of the proletariat a conduct more perfect (?) than that of Jesus? Where is it written that the words of Jesus have a more normative character than his deeds?

That Jesus used physical violence is a fact that cannot be denied. "And having made a scourge out of cords he drove them all out of the temple" (John 2:15). The aorist participle signifies here the instrumentality or mode by which the action of the main verb is carried out. What John really says here is, he whipped them all out of the temple. Or does flabby theology think he exhorted them out of the temple?

And it is historically certain that he could not have driven them out by himself, so at this juncture the evangelists must be omitting something. In the first place, the traders were many. And in the second place they had guards. Without a doubt Jesus had placed himself at the head of a burly group of his followers in an action which can only be characterized as an assault on the temple. By what authority do you deny, precisely to the proletariat, in the name of Christianity, the legitimacy of a type of action performed by Jesus Christ himself?

BIBLIOGRAPHY

Binzler, Johannes. In *Lexikon für Theologie und Kirche*. Frieburg im Breisgau: Herder, 1957–1968, s. v. "Vollkammenheit," 10: 865–66.

Bornkamm, Günther. *Jesus von Nazaret*. 2nd ed. Stuttgart: Kohlhammer, 1965. [Eng., *Jesus of Nazareth*. New York: Harper & Row, 1960].

Brown, Raymond E. *The Gospel according to John*. Anchor Bible 29 and 29A. New York: Doubleday, 1966, 1970.

Elliger, Karl. *Das Buch der zwölf kleinen Propheten*. Das Alte Testament Deutsch 25. 6th ed. Göttingen: Vandenhoeck, 1967.

Grundmann, Walter. *Das Evangelium nach Markus*. 4th ed. Berlin: Evangelische Verlagsanstalt, 1968.

Hauck Friedrich. In *Theologische Wörterbuch zum neuen Testament* (TWNT). Ed. Gerhard Kittel and Gerhard Friedrich. Stuttgart: Kohlhammer, 1933–1978, s. v. "ploutos," etc., 6:316–30 [Eng., *Theological Dictionary of the New Testament* (TDNT). Trans. and ed. Geoffrey W. Bromiley. 9 vols. Grand Rapids, Mich.: Eerdmans, 1964–1970, 6:318–32].

Jeremias, Joachim. In TWNT, s. v. "hades," 1:146–49 [Eng., TDNT, 1:146–49].

———. In TWNT, s. v. "parádeisos," 5:765–73 [Eng., TDNT, 5: 763–71].

Kraus, Hans-Joachim. *Psalmen*. 2 vols. 3rd ed. Neukirchen: Neukirchener Verlag, 1966.

Miranda, José Porfirio. *Cambio de estructuras: immoralidad de la moral occidental*. Mexico City, 1971. [German trans., *Von der unmoral gegenwärtiger Structuran: Dargestellt am Beispiel Mexiko*. Trans. Annalise Swartzer de Ruiz. Wuppertal: Jugenddiest-Verlag, 1973].

———. *El cristianismo de Marx*. Mexico City, 1978. [Eng., *Marx against the Marxists: The Christian Humanism of Karl Marx*. Trans. John Drury. Maryknoll, N.Y.: Orbis Books, 1980].

————. *Marx y la biblia: Crítica a la filosofía de la opresión.* Salamanca: Sígueme, 1971 [Eng., *Marx and the Bible: A Critique of the Philosophy of Oppression.* Trans. John Eagleson. Maryknoll, N.Y.: Orbis Books, 1974].

————. *El ser y el mesías.* Salamanca: Sígueme, 1973 [Revised for Eng., *Being and the Messiah: The Message of St. John.* Trans. John Eagleson. Maryknoll, N.Y.: Orbis Books, 1977].

Schlier, Heinrich. *Die Zeit der Kirche.* 3rd ed. Freiburg im Breisgau: Herder, 1962.

Schnackenburg, Rudolf. "Evangelische Räte I: In der Shrift." In *Lexikon für Theologie und Kirche*, 3:1246.

Schneider, Johannes. In TWNT s. v. "stauros," 7:572-84 [TNDT, 7:572-80].

Schweizer, Eduard. *Das Evangelium nach Markus.* Das Neue Testament Deutsch 1. Göttingen: Vandenhoeck, 1967 [Eng., *The Good News according to Mark.* Trans. Donald Madrig. Richmond: John Knox Press, 1970].

Smith, C. W. F. *The Jesus of the Parables.* Philadelphia: Westminster, 1948.

Strack, Hermann, and Paul Billerbeck. *Kommentar zum neuen Testament aus Talmud und Midrash.* 6 vols. Munich: C. H. Beck, 1922-63.

Taylor, Vincent, ed. *The Gospel according to St. Mark.* 2nd ed. London: Macmillan, and New York: St. Martin's, 1966.

Weiser, Artur. *Die Psalmen.* 2 vols. Das Alte Testament Deutsch 14 and 15. Göttingen: Vandenhoeck, 1950 [Eng., *The Psalms: A Commentary.* Trans. Herbert Hartwell. Philadelphia: Westminster, 1962].

Westerman, Claus. *Das Buch Jesaja, Kap. 40-66.* Das Alte Testament Deutsch 19. Göttingen: Vandenhoeck, 1966 [Eng., *Isaiah 40-66: A Commentary.* Philadelphia: Westminster, 1969].

Wolff, Hans Walter. *Joel und Amos, Biblische Kommentar.* Neukirchen: Neukirchener Verlag, 1969 [Eng., *Joel and Amos: A Commentary on the Prophets Joel and Amos.* Philadelphia: Fortress, 1977].

Zahn, Theodor. *Das Evangelium des Mattäus.* 3rd ed. Leipzig: A. Deichert, 1910.

INDEX OF SCRIPTURAL REFERENCES

OLD TESTAMENT

Genesis		18:21	49	24:23	74
1:27	56	20:12	75	25:36	54
2:7	56	21:12	74	25:37	54
9:6	74	21:15	74		
13:2	21	21:16	74	**Numbers**	
37:17	66	21:17	74, 75, 76	11:31	66
37:26	49	22:24	54	22:24	66
41ff	31	32:7	66		
42:15	66	33:1	66	**Deuteronomy**	
43:34	35	33:5	66	4:34	75
50:25	66			5:15	75
		Leviticus		6:13	64
Exodus		6:2-4	37	7:16	64
6:6	75	19:4	64	7:19	75
11:1	66	19:13	37	9:12	66
13:3	66	19:18	76	10:20	64
13:19	66	20:2	74	15:11	59
17:4	74	20:27	74	23:19	54
17:12	66	24:14	74	26:8	75

81

THE APOCRYPHA AND PSEUDEPIGRAPHA

NEW TESTAMENT